The TRUTH Set Us Free

TWENTY FORMER NUNS TELL THEIR STORIES

Richard Bennett, Editor, with Mary Hertel

WinePress Publishing
MUKILTEO, WA 98275

The Truth Set Us Free
Copyright © 1997 Richard Bennett

Published by WinePress Publishing
PO Box 1406
Mukilteo, WA 98275

Cover by **DENHAM**DESIGN, Everett, WA

Printed in the United States of America.

ISBN 1-57921-067-8
Library of Congress Catalog Card Number: 97-61892

Contents

Foreword 5

Editorial Comment 7

Acknowledgements 9

1. **Jacqueline Kassar:** 11
   From a Nun's Convent to Biblical Conversion

2. **Lolly Harding:** 15
   *A Medical Nun/Air Evac Nun's Story of Conversion
   to the Truth*

3. **Eileen Donnelly:** 21
   Led by the Shepherd

4. **Nancy Hohman:** .29
   Finding True Freedom in Christ: My Testimony

5. **Rita A. Riel:** 35
   From Religion to Relationship

6. **Mary C. Hertel:** 47
   The Unsearchable Ways of God

7. **Mary Ann Pakiz:** .61
   God's Word Needs No Authority Other Than Itself

8. **Jo Ellen Kaminski:** 69
   His Banner Over Me Is Love

9. **Amy Bentley:** 75
   The Conversion of a Catholic Nun: My Return to Christ

10. **Rocio P. Zwirner:** .81
    The Woman at the Well

11. **Alicia Simpson:** 99
Alicia: My Search for Peace, a Nun's Story

12. **Sophia Tekien:** 107
And the Truth Made Me Free

13. **Donna Spader Shire:** 119
Mother's Vocation and God's Grace

14. **Lucille Poulin:** 123
The Truth Shall Make You Free!

15. **Doreen Eberhardt (D'Antonio):** 133
This Is My Story

16. **Eileen M. Doran:** 139
A Labyrinthian Way

17. **Wilma Sullivan:** 155
Ex-Nun Finds Peace with God

18. **Peggy O'Neill:** 159
I Had Never Heard the True Gospel

19. **Karlene Lynn:** 175
All I Wanted to Know Was to Know Jesus

20. **Helene Hart:** 179
From Confusion to the Truth of Scripture

Epilogue 183

Foreword

Woven throughout the accounts of twenty former nuns is a search for God within the confines of religious life ordained by the Catholic Church. It was there that their families and personal conviction said they could know and serve Him best. Yet, His transforming presence eluded them. Although each story was written separately, spanning England, Ireland, Scotland, Spain, the United States, South America, and Canada, a unifying theme is clear:

"You shall know the truth and the truth shall set you free."

The meaning of this freedom and how it is manifest is fleshed out in a myriad of experiences evaluated in the light of Truth. Through unique situations, each woman came to recognize the personal, loving, dynamic presence of God in her own life. The divine call is revealed and answers provided for nagging questions and aching emptiness. Statements from two different accounts expose the void:

"Religion had offered nothing and the 'lust of the flesh, the lust of the eyes, and the pride of life' made for more discontent."

"What caused the strong feelings of emptiness, so acute that something was not answering my need?"

The message is as contemporary as the day it is read. Their search is every man's search. Twenty different, yet biblically identical resolutions present the only Way that sets anyone free from whatever bondage enslaves him—the Way through faith in the completed work of Jesus Christ.

MARY HERTEL, September 2, 1997

Editorial Comment

We have attempted to select testimonies which reflect the biblical principles that salvation is by grace alone, through faith alone, in Christ alone, on the authority of the Bible alone, so that God alone should have the glory. This has been done with a pastoral purpose: the salvation of souls. We have not produced a theological manual, nor is it the intention of the editor or those who have assisted in compiling the book to endorse every doctrinal statement made in the testimonies. We do, however, praise the Lord for the unity of faith expressed among us.

For further information or assistance please contact:

Mary Hertel
18320 Tilton Lane
Brookfield, WI 53045
USA
Tel. 414-784-5998 Fax 414-784-5961

Or

Richard Bennett
P.O. Box 55353
Portland, OR 97238-5353
USA
Telephone and FAX: (503) 257-5995
E-Mail: bereanbennett@juno.com

Acknowledgements

The testimonies themselves give thanks to God for His grace that made the account of each life possible. With thanksgiving to the Lord, we wish also to express heartfelt thanks to His faithful servants who have made this collection possible.

Great aid in publishing this book has been given by J. A. Tony Tosti and Westminster Institute of Vancouver, Washington. We truly appreciate their help.

We are grateful to William H. M. MacKenzie of Christian Focus Publications, Ltd. (Geanies House Fearn, Tain, Ross-shire, IV20 1TX, Scotland, UK) for permission to summarize the excellent book, *Alicia - My Search for Peace*. We want also to express our thanks to Bob Jones, Chancellor of Bob Jones University, for permission to use paragraphs one through three and six through eleven of Wilma Sullivan's testimony.

It has been a great joy to us to work together with Bob DeKoning, who has given hours and hours of faithful service at the computer. In our hour of need in changing computer systems, Sylvia Thompson gave graciously her dedicated professional aid, for which we express deep thanks.

Jacqueline Kassar

From a Nun's Convent to Biblical Conversion

Forty-five years of my life were spent as a Roman Catholic, twenty-two of them as a nun in an enclosed convent dedicated to adoration, reparation and suffering. I believed it was a nun's calling to be a miniature savior of the world, like Jesus Christ.

My Decision to be a Nun

After attending Catholic elementary school for eight years and memorizing catechism, which is the Roman Catholic textbook, I believed in my heart that a family having a son or daughter become a priest or nun would receive God's favor and special blessings. I decided to enter the convent when I was old enough to leave home. This was my goal while I was still in my teens. On my twenty-first birthday, 1954, I entered the convent against my parent's wishes. My belief in my calling to be a nun superseded my parent's vehement opposition.

Even though it broke my heart to leave my parents, I consoled myself in the fact that I was doing God's will by making this sacrifice for the salvation of my family and all those outside the Catholic faith who, I believed, were doomed to hell.

Convent Life

At first, I was in awe of the solitude, structural beauty and peacefulness the convent seemed to have. I was taught to do penances such as sleeping on a board, prostrating myself at the door of the dining room as an act of humiliation, and beating myself as a means of appeasing God's wrath. This taught me to believe in a punishing, unapproachable and unloving God. I feared Him at every turn of my life. As time went on, emptiness filled my heart and hopelessness engulfed me. I became depressed, often crying while I raged with anger at authority and hatred for the rules and customs of the convent that were so very cruel. My body developed all kinds of illnesses and I found myself with a tremor that only Valium could help. All the time the medication was dulling my mind and taking away my ability to think and reason.

My Yearning to Know God

I was so hungry to know that God loved me and so wanting to know Him that I started reading mystical writings which taught that

you could attain mystical union with God, thereby achieving supernatural knowledge of Him which leads to total holiness. This path directed me to super-naturalize not only the Bible and Jesus, but anything to do with my religious life. Step by step I lost my ability to reason and deal with real-ity, for reality was too painful for me to face.

"I begin in awe and wonder"

Answered Prayer

Still feeling hopeless and so despondent, I cried out to God. In His mercy and grace He heard my prayers. In 1975, a distant cousin who had become a Christian brought an evangelist, who was visit-ing New York, to the convent. He was holding a street meeting at a nearby Catholic parish. I received permission to go and for the first time I heard the true Gospel. It certainly was **Good News!** *"For God so loved the world, that he gave his only begotten Son, that whosoever believeth in him should not perish, but have everlasting life"* (John 3:16). I learned that Jesus died for my sins, past, present and future. When I accepted Him as my Lord and Savior and repented of my sins, He made my dead spirit alive and began a personal relationship between the Lord and myself. This is the gift of God to those who believe, *"For by grace are ye saved through faith; and that not of yourselves: it is the gift of God: Not of works, lest any man should boast"* (Ephesians 2: 8, 9). How important it is to know that we must **individually** trust and believe in Him. *"That if thou shalt confess with thy mouth the Lord Jesus, and shalt believe in thine heart that God hath raised him from the dead, thou shalt be saved"* (Romans 10: 9).

My Life After Hearing the Gospel

After personally accepting Jesus Christ as my Lord and Savior, I started to read my Bible and pray directly to God. In 1977, I left the convent and started on my quest to know the truth. God's Word became my only authority and everything else was measured against the Bible. But this was just the beginning. I did not realize the serious harm false doctrines and beliefs had created in my body and mind.

Through a friend I met a Christian who helped me see that being a doer of the Word brings healing to the body and clarity to the mind, for through the new birth we can have the mind of Christ. It has not been an easy road, but it has been one filled with God's love and blessing.

God's Faithfulness

The Lord has been faithful to me in the promises of His Word. He promised to *"restore the years that the locusts have eaten"* (Joel 2:25), enabling me to begin a new life filled with joy and a true inner peace that neither the world nor religion can give.

It is my hope and prayer that I might have the privilege of sharing the love and goodness of God by telling all who will hear that He has a plan for each life and He is faithful to accomplish that plan when we receive the gift of salvation by believing in His Son.

" Eye hath not seen, nor ear heard, neither have entered into the heart of man, the things which God hath prepared for them that love him ."
(1Corinthians 2:9)

"The Lord is faithful day by day"

13

Lolly Harding

A Medical Nun/Air Evac Nurse's Story of Conversion to the Truth

Callous treatment of a skilled drug-addicted nun-surgeon by her peer group in the Catholic Medical Missionary Order caused me, a dedicated nun, to become disillusioned. Within every person lies a marvelous adventure story of his life. Here is my story and the three torturous, separate paths I took on my journey toward peace and reconciliation with God. My first path was that of religion as a medical missionary nun for thirteen years. Then I searched in vain for fulfillment as a United States Air Force nurse for six and a half years. Finally, on the third path, as a married homemaker on a Texas ranch, I found *"the peace that passeth all understanding"* when I received Jesus Christ as my Savior. I can now say with Jeremiah 31:3, *"The Lord hath appeared of old unto me, saying, Yea, I have loved thee with an everlasting love: therefore with lovingkindness have I drawn thee."*

My First Path: Religion

I was raised in a devout Roman Catholic family of six children in Cascade, Iowa, and entered a medical missionary order at age eighteen. In my idealistic youth, my goal was to help less fortunate people. After two and a half years of strict religious training, I professed vows of poverty, chastity and obedience. After receiving a nursing degree from prestigious Georgetown University School of Nursing in Washington, DC, I was sent to the mission field in Rawalpindi, Pakistan. My experiences in the convent included working in a hospital for Muslims and a tour attending pregnant girls in a home for unwed mothers in Philadelphia.

In one case Sister Barbara, a skilled surgeon, was literally worked to death by unselfishly attending Muslim women. Since in Pakistan no male surgeon could touch a Muslim woman to perform needed operations, Sister Barbara, the only woman surgeon at her clinic, worked excessively long shifts to the point of exhaustion. When she began taking Demerol to keep going, her associates looked the other way. Soon she was a confirmed addict. When I met Sister Barbara, she was hopelessly addicted, left to wander about the hospital grounds and was neither given treatment nor sent away from the source of drugs, but simply forgotten.

"The mission field"

After thirteen years, being psychologically unable to adjust to convent life as a nun, I requested and received a dispensation from my vows. At age thirty-two, I left the convent with a nurse's license, a release from my vows, a new conservative suit, and fare home. The main reason for leaving was great disillusionment with the hypocrisy and lack of love among the nuns. I also found it a psychologically sterile, unfulfilling life; the convent rules imposed abnormal, emotionally lonely conditions. Lonely, lonely, I wanted to relate to **someone** and, eventually, to **get out**.

My Second Path: USAF Nurse Corps

Shortly thereafter, I joined the USAF Nurse Corps as a captain, originally based in California. This pathway in my life was exciting and filled with new worldly vanities. Like an uncorked bottle, I threw myself into these pursuits with the same gusto I had as a nun. I learned to drink, have sex, buy luxuries and taste the pleasures that the world offers.

On the surface, my assignments were interesting with a tour of duty at Travis Air Force Base, California, then two years as a flight nurse in Yokota Air Force Base, Japan. This was during the Vietnam War. I served as an air evac nurse, attending wounded military men on their evacuation from Vietnam battlefields through Pacific hospital stops to home via Alaska or California. I saw the world and lived a wild life for six and a half years. During all of this I managed to sear my Catholic conscience and justify my lifestyle. I had no inner peace and the void in my soul grew even greater. Religion had offered nothing and the *"lust of the flesh, the lust of the eyes and the pride of life"* made for *more* discontent. I found myself running to confess my many transgressions to a priest, but with no **real** repentance.

"In the USAF Nurse Corps"

A Third Path: Marriage

During my last tour as a Major at the air base near Del Rio, Texas, I met and married a retired veterinarian-rancher. I resigned my Air Force commission and began living the third chapter of my life as a ranch housewife, thirty-five miles from town. Although I was "living in sin", I was a nominal Catholic, continuing to attend Mass, to pray to Mary, and to practice all the rituals of the Church. My husband was a divorced Protestant, so I was not supposed to receive the sacraments (whatever good that does). This supposed transgression was viewed by the Catholic Church as much worse than all the past years of party and sexual perfidy with married men, etc. After all, those sins were absolved by the priests. My soul was not at peace even though I led a quiet life on a beautiful Texas ranch. I continued to feel a restlessness in my soul. My marriage was not enough to fill the longing in my spirit.

My Introduction to the Truth

After four years of married life, I attended a family reunion in Iowa. Unknown to me, my older brother had gotten saved. He spent the rest of his life witnessing to our family as well as to others who were blinded to the truth by their devout Roman Catholic position. My sisters warned me about my "Bible thumping" brother before I arrived. Due to my Jesuit indoctrination, it was now my duty to straighten him out. My brother gathered the whole family around the dining table with an open King James Bible before him. I shut my mouth, put down my martini glass, and listened to him with astonishment and confusion. He told the family that there is *"one Mediator between God and men, the man Christ Jesus"* (1 Timothy 2:5) and that we were all headed for **hell**.

He said that we were trusting in our Roman Catholic Church, worshiping Mary (a fake substitute for Jesus Christ), celebrating the Mass (a cannibalistic mockery of the death of Jesus Christ), and observing the Catholic sacramental life with its many anti-biblical doctrines such as Purgatory. According to Catholic teaching, Purgatory is the place you go after death to burn until God decides you have suffered enough to enter heaven. What a crock! It is not in the Bible! My brother emphasized that salvation was a free gift, the only thing necessary on man's part is *believing* on Jesus Christ as Savior. *"That if thou shalt confess with thy mouth the Lord Jesus and shalt believe in thine heart that God hath raised him from the dead, thou shalt be saved"* (Romans 10:9). There is no need for self-righteous works to earn your way to heaven as taught by the Catholic doctrine. This was a shocking concept and I was confused, to say the least.

The next day my brother again opened the Bible and showed me the fallacy of the Catholic position in almost everything I had held as infallible truth for forty-four years. Psychologically, I had such a trust and attachment to Holy Mother Church that I naturally resisted the obvious truth that my brother presented. I returned home to Texas still in a state of confusion. How could the Church which I had loved and trusted completely be so totally anti-biblical and full of lies? I had never dared to question the Church's claim to be the exclusive way (conduit) to forgiveness of sin and the key to heaven or hell. My wise brother advised me to read the Gospel of John and the Epistle of Paul to the Romans which states so clearly, *"God commendeth his love toward us in that, while we were yet sinners, Christ died for us"* (Romans 5:8) and *"Therefore being justified by faith, we have peace with God through our Lord Jesus Christ"* (Romans 5:1). He also quoted Ephesians 2:8-9, *"For by grace are ye saved through faith; and that not of yourselves; it is the gift of God; not of works, lest any man should boast."*

True Liberty

From deep within my soul, I cried to my Savior to save me from my own self-righteousness. The *"peace that passeth all understanding"*

"My husband and me on our Texas ranch"

flooded my being for the first time in my life. The shackles of all those years in bondage to the Catholic Church slowly crumbled, and I began to know the true liberty of a child of God. I was a new creature in Christ. This new birth in Christ is the most wonderful of miracles. After studying my King James Bible for years, this miracle has become clearer. The gift of salvation, which is eternal life, is not a **process** but rather a one-time birth into the family of God.

An Urgent Plea

My dear Catholic friends, I beg you to do as I did. Come to Jesus Christ as a lost soul and trust His blood atonement at Calvary to pay for your sins. He took your place on the Cross to pay for the sins of the whole world. Receive this gift of eternal life from Him by your acceptance of His complete payment of your sins by His death, burial and resurrection. The Catholic Church has deprived you of the simple plan of salvation and has substituted a tortuous plan of works. There is no need for the pagan sacrifice you make at Mass or the futile confessing of sins to a priest. Jesus Christ awaits you, as He did me when I was a lost Roman Catholic, to believe on Him for salvation. Once saved, the Lord does not abandon us. There is provision for learning and growth in His Word. *"Rightly dividing the Word of truth"* is the only protection from the many cults of our day which sound so logical and attractive. The Lord is faithful to provide all we need.

Eileen Donnelly

Led by the Shepherd

"The Lord is my Shepherd, I shall not want...He leadeth me in the paths of righteousness for His name's sake." Psalm 23: 1, 3

My name is Eileen Donnelly. On July 5, 1911, I was born in a small village just outside of Montreal. Along with two brothers and two sisters, I was brought up in a staunchly Catholic home. In school, I learned the fundamental teachings of the Church given by Catholic nuns. In July, 1928, at the age of seventeen, I decided to join my teachers and became a teaching sister myself. I spent the next fifty-five years in a convent, where I was totally absorbed in my work, and I loved it. Teaching assignments were in Chicago, Illinois; Detroit, Michigan; Windsor, Ontario; Silver Spring, Maryland; and Montreal, Quebec. I was happy and my life flowed on like a river. Oh, there were ups and downs, but it never entered my mind to waver or to look back.

Being Led into a New Way

It wasn't until around 1972 that I came into regular contact with "born again" believers through the Charismatic Movement. I had never owned a Bible or heard of being "born again" or of the "gifts of the Spirit". I had much to learn. Reluctantly, I began going to prayer

"As a teaching sister, St. Paul's school"

meetings, urged on by a companion at work. At this time, after thirty-eight years of teaching, I was engaged in social work.

What attracted me most and fed my heart and soul for weeks was an understanding of the Lord's desire that we come to know and love Him more intimately. This struck a responsive chord in me and kept me going to the meetings where I met believers who were using the gifts God had given them. Through them I was led to join a small prayer group where, little by little, I was learning the Lord's Way.

Resisting the Lead

Looking back over these years, I can laugh at myself as I recognize the gentle nudging the shepherd used to draw me to Himself and His flock. Had the leader of this small prayer group not been the man he was, I would have dropped out because the years that followed were the most crucifying ones I have ever lived.

A Catholic sister in the group shared with me that the Lord showed her that my theology was wrong. No details were given and I felt stranded and alone, like a lost sheep, unable to help myself. I wanted to know in what areas I was wrong but, for the moment, there were no answers. The Lord has His own way of guiding and it was only by degrees, step by step, that He led me to His truth. I know that if it had not been done His way, the shock might have shattered my faith completely.

The first breakdown was concerning the Mass, where I found my soul's nourishment, because I firmly believed that Christ was physically present in the Eucharist. From the age of sixteen, I had never voluntarily missed daily communion. My entire religious life was centered around the Eucharist. When the road became too rough for me, I went to my tabernacled Christ for support and guidance and despite my ignorance regarding real presence there, I know without a shadow of a doubt that He overlooked my ignorance and supplied my need. Many times I had tangible answers to prayer.

One day, as I prayed, I began to question in this manner, "I have been receiving Christ in communion daily for years now, then why am I not a saint today? Why is He not more real to me? Why do I have to look to friends for the love and support I need to carry on in this religious life?" I was thus running risks that could have meant my ruin had not the Lord's protective love shielded me. "Why do I not know the Lord experientially if He is really and truly present in the Eucharist that I receive daily?" I felt cheated, let down, as though something powerfully needed was missing in my life. Was I guilty in some unknown way? What caused this strong feeling of emptiness, so acute that something was not answering my need?

Today I know that my Shepherd was slowly, patiently leading me to the discovery that He is not physically present in the Eucharist as I had been taught so deceptively. In His perfect timing, I could accept it more easily. Through the leader of the prayer group, himself a former Catholic who had gone through the darkness and come into the light, the Lord taught me where my belief was wrong. In true Irish fashion, I rebelled at the very thought that believing in the real presence in the Eucharist was wrong. Based on the words of the Bible, I argued, *"Except ye eat the flesh of the Son of man, and drink his blood, ye have no life in you. Whoso eateth my flesh and drinketh my blood, hath eternal life; and I will raise him up at the last day."* How could I be wrong? The leader always said, "Stick by the Book, lean on the Word." As Paul said, *"But though we, or an angel from heaven, preach any other gospel unto you than that which we have preached unto you, let him be accursed"* (Galatians 1:9). If it is not in the Book, do not accept it even if it is an angel who tells you. How could I accept this? It was in the Book. To say that I fought it is putting it mildly!

If Christ was not physically present in the Eucharist, then the bottom was falling out of my religious life. What was left? I was shattered, but the Lord gave me the strength to not walk away. I stayed and fought on, prayed, and studied until I accepted in obedience because the one who was teaching me was a sincere, obedient follower of the Lord. He had traveled this road before me and if he had survived and loved the Lord as he does, then why couldn't I? However, in no mistakable terms, I told the Lord, "You will have to teach me Yourself," and he did just that!

"In true Irish fashion, 1977 at 40 years old"

Drawn to the Shepherd

One error after the other was shown to me until I realized just how wrong my theology had been. The rest was easier to accept, for I can see it all so plainly now. I wondered how I could have been

23

so blind. When all your life you have been taught that the Catholic Church is the only true Church and that all others are wrong, you do not go out on a witchhunt searching for error. It simply does not occur to you that you are being deceived.

The leader of our group said to me one day, "Eileen, why did you not search for the truth?" Inside my feathers were ruffled and I told him, "Today, why don't you start hunting for a different answer to two plus two? It doesn't enter your mind because you have taken for granted that the answer, four, is correct." In the past I never questioned the doctrine I had been taught. Not so today! I argue with priests and nuns as I never would have dared to do years ago. In the process, I realize that unless the Lord removes the scales from their eyes they simply cannot see the truth, for they are in total darkness. Jesus said, *"No man can come to Me, except the Father which hath sent Me draw him; and I will raise him up on the last day"* (John 7:44).

Biblical Understanding

For some years I did not own a Bible so I was ignorant of the truth it contained. If at a prayer meeting someone asked me to read Psalm Twenty-three, I could have easily begun searching in Genesis. An example is devotion to Mary and the saints. In the community to which I belonged, December 8th, the Feast of the Immaculate Conception is celebrated with pomp and splendor. For years I sang in convent choirs repeating again and again the words of the Magnificat, "My soul magnifies the Lord and my spirit rejoices in God my Savior." Never once did it enter my mind to question the words *"in God my Savior"*, yet the truth was there for everyone to see. Why had I never awakened to this discrepancy? How could Mary be conceived immaculate and still proclaim Christ to be her Savior? If she needed a Savior, then she was a sinner like all the rest of us, as good a woman as she must have been. Besides, Christ said He was like us in all things, except sin. Our mothers were not conceived immaculate, neither was His. Christ also refutes her immaculate conception when He said, *"Verily I say unto you, Among them that are born of women there hath not risen a greater than John the Baptist"* (Matthew 11:11). Mary was living at that time.

More and more of the false teachings came crashing down. What about the Lourdes' apparition that claimed to be the Immaculate Conception? Mary would not have lied! Then the one who did appear was the deceiver, the father of lies! Yet, Catholics have been obliged to believe this lie of 1854 because of the dogma proclaimed by our "infallible" popes. Paul's teaching in Galatians 1:8 speaks about such deception, *"But though we, or an angel from heaven, preach any other gospel unto you than that which we have preached to you, let him be accursed."* Now I could see clearly! The same holds true for the dogma of the Assumption of Mary into heaven, proclaimed by Pius the XII. Attempts of popes to proclaim "Mary, Mediatrix of all graces" completely contradicts the Word of God which teaches that Jesus is the only Mediator between God and men (1Timothy 2: 5-6).

Next came the question of purgatory and all the Masses that are supposed to relieve and ransom souls from their sufferings. None of this is biblical. One example from the Bible that exposes this false teaching is the thief on the cross to whom Christ said, *"This day thou shalt be with me in Paradise."* A whole life of sin was washed away in a moment, as the thief recognized and believed in Jesus Christ and was given the promise of eternal life in Paradise that very day. Even Catholicism taught that the soul appears before Christ immediately after death and is judged. If saved, the soul is admitted to heaven and if lost it is condemned to hell. In view of this teaching, where is the logic in urging the faithful to have Masses said again and again for years? One that is saved does not need them and one that is lost cannot benefit by them since out of hell there is no redemption.

What about the Mass itself? It is condemned in Hebrews 10:14, *"for by one offering He hath perfected forever them are sanctified."* The Bible also makes it clear that *"only God can forgive sin"*. We are to confess our sins directly to Him. Jesus Christ is our High Priest and everyone who believes in Him shares in this royal priesthood. There is no need for indulgences, *"and the blood of Jesus Christ cleanseth us from all sin"* (1 John 1:7). Jesus paid our sin debt in full. The list of teachings that are contrary to God's Word goes on and on.

Personal Direction

A personal direction from God's Word was given to me in Isaiah 48: 20, *"Go ye forth of Babylon, flee ye from the Chaldeans, with a voice of singing declare ye, tell this, utter it even to the end of the earth; say ye, The Lord redeemed his servant Jacob."* Confirmation from others also made it clear that I was to leave the convent. It was December 18th, 1982. Within a week I had written a nine-page letter to the authorities of my community detailing for them the errors I had discovered in the teachings of the Catholic Church, giving them Biblical references to back up my statements and telling them that the day had come when I could no longer continue living a life so blatantly contrary to the teachings of the Bible. Therefore, as of December 31st, 1982, I was no longer to be considered a member of their community and asked to be released from any legal obligation towards them. I could not continue where there was only ritualistic performance.

I was told that Rome would possibly not consider my given reasons sufficient to release me. But I assured them that, if necessary, I would take up my petition with Rome myself and I meant what I said. Rome officially granted my request on June 10th, 1983, but I belonged to the Lord long before when I accepted Him as my Savior. He became my Shepherd and my life belonged to Him. No longer would I follow the traditions of man.

Care for My Every Need

A member of the Apostolic Fellowship in Verdun, Quebec, called the social agency where I had been working for the past thirteen years, inquiring about an association for patients suffering from Parkinson's disease. After giving the requested information, I mentioned to the caller that according to her statements she was rendering service above and beyond the call of duty and added that the Lord had said, *"what you do for one of these, you do unto me."* Immediately she said, "You are a born-again Christian, aren't you?" I admitted that I am and she insisted that we meet.

The following Sunday I went to the Apostolic Church, met my telephone friend and have been attending Sunday services there ever since. Again, the Lord was leading me, taking care of my every need.

On July 8th, 1984, I requested to be baptized after pondering over the baptism I had received in the Catholic Church when I was four days old. I now realized that this, too, was not according to God's Word. I was baptized by Pastor John Kristensen on July 10th, 1984.

My On-Going Mission

My on-going mission among other things is to go to the blind and the weak. Frequently I pray for those I left behind in the convent that they will be brought to the light of His truth. The Lord has and continues to fulfill in my life the message in a hymn that says, "Great is Thy faithfulness...Morning by morning new mercies I see...**All I have needed, Thy hand has provided. Great is Thy faithfulness, Lord, unto me.**"

"My work and prayer corner"

Since I left my working days, after almost fifty-five years of teaching and then back to college to qualify for social service for the next twenty years, at age eighty I am still not unemployed. Instead I am busy as a beaver in the Lord's work of getting out the Good News of redemption through the blood of Jesus Christ. This is done by lengthy explanatory letters sent to those I learn of by the newscasts, newspapers, word of mouth, phone calls, etc. The Lord brings His work to me. Here are two examples. I saw in a local paper the picture of a "hooker" who worked for ten years in the West, now dying of AIDS. She was being cared for in a local home. The paper announced that she was looking forward to her marriage to a man in the same boat as herself. They both looked like death warmed over. I recognized the name of the place where she and her fiancé were staying. Thinking of how compassionately our beloved Lord brought Mary Magdalene to Himself, I prayed for direction to write to this dying woman. The newspaper said she was looking forward to her wedding day. The home had made her dress, ordered her cake, etc., and she was joyful once more, but she had very little time to live.

In my letter I referred to the anticipated joy she felt because of her wedding day and asked her if I could tell her of a greater joy by far, one that would never end. Then I launched out into a minute explanation of what it means to be born-again and the joy in heaven's celebration as a stray lamb is found by the Shepherd. Soon after the letter was sent, the same newspaper reported that she had called off the wedding and returned home to her mother. The letter may well have been used by the Lord for sharing with her former lover, her mother, and others.

A second example was a newspaper report of a woman with Lou Gehrig's disease. She also had little time left to live. Her comment was, "At least I'll have time to prepare for my death." No address was given but the Roman Catholic priest came to bring her communion so I called the parish church. When I asked for her address, explaining that I belonged to a prayer group and wanted to send her a card with wishes and prayers, I was told they never give addresses. So I asked that if the greeting was sent to the rectory, could the priest on his next visit give it to her? This was acceptable. In the well-sealed envelope was a detailed explanation of the system of works taught by the Catholic Church that gives no assurance for eternity until you are face to face in judgment. This was followed by the Good News which is so different. Your debt was paid in full by Jesus' death on Calvary when His blood washed away our all our sin. Assurance of salvation is available **if we believe and accept the offered salvation.**

The Harvest is Great

I have found ways to get the truth of salvation to members of government, sharing in terms they cannot rebuke except by suppressing the truth (Romans 1: 18). A visiting pastor from England requested that I write my testimony and he had it published in his country. Several churches have invited me to give my testimony and with my pastor's approbation, much detail has been shared with them. We can only faithfully present the truth of salvation when we have the opportunity and leave the results to the Lord. It is a privilege to work in the Lord's harvest.

A Life of Thanksgiving

I want my testimony to be one of praise and thanksgiving to my magnificent Shepherd for His mercy and love towards me. He led the whole way and all I had to do was obey and follow His leading. Among so many things I am most grateful for is the fact that when He called me, He gave me the strength and the will to obey immediately without looking back or questioning the future as to how I would manage alone in this world. Though I had cut myself off from all material security, I knew He was there and I had nothing to fear. He would never leave me nor forsake me. He has been there every inch of the way. There is joy and peace in my walk with the Lord. As time goes on, I am closer and closer to Him and there is a longing to know Him better, love Him more, and follow where He leads.

Nancy Hohman

Finding True Freedom in Christ: My Testimony

Like any teenager, the dream of my life was to have a family and home of my own. I attended public school during the week and catechism class on Saturdays. A Franciscan Order of sisters taught the catechism and one sister in particular played an important part in my life. She invited me to join her in celebrating her twenty-five years of dedication. Little did I know that this was a fork in the road that would bring about radical changes in my life.

Convent Boarding School

I attended that celebration and my life took a different turn that day when I sensed God saying, "Come follow Me." I thought God was calling me to become a nun, so I completed my high school years at the convent boarding school and began preparation for a life of service to the King of Heaven.

From Certainty to Uncertainty

For a while the conviction that God had called me helped me overcome the doubt and obstacles that I faced in this new life. As time went by, however, my eyes and heart were opened to the futility of rote prayers and rituals. I questioned my sinfulness and the sinfulness of all of us nuns who were supposed to be so holy. The door to freedom would often swing open, but across the threshold uncertainty was written. Each choice to leave or decision to stay caused me wrenching pain and great sorrow.

On one occasion, I had made the decision to leave when the former president of the order and a sister friend of mine, asked me

"Preparing for life as a nun"

if I was absolutely certain this was the right decision. My response was a flood of tears, as I felt unsure about God's will for me. I resigned myself to stay, supposing it must be God's will.

Ministry in the Mississippi Delta

Then God led me into a ministry among the poor in the Mississippi Delta. On my flight to Mississippi, viewing the small patch-work fields from the vantage of the sky made them truly seem like God's country. In the Delta, I saw first-hand what faith was as I observed the lives of God's people. One preacher who was in his nineties struck me by his vast knowledge of the Bible by heart. As his human eyes grew dim, remembrance of the Lord's Word was like music and balm to his soul. He took great joy and delight in praising the Lord for all His goodness and looked forward to their special union at death. His assurance of being with Jesus made all in life worthwhile to him. It was a puzzle to me how he could be certain that his eternity was secure.

An elderly woman shared her daily prayer with us. "Each time

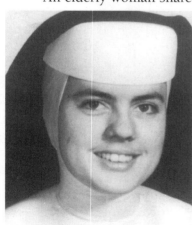

"Clothed with religion, I was puzzled by the assurance of others"

I awake to a new day, I thank the Lord that the four walls of my room were not the walls of my coffin and that these sheets upon my bed were not my winding cloth and thank the Lord for the gift of another day." Such faith was unfamiliar to me. If I had been in her position, my heart would not have praised God, but blamed Him for my circumstances. Where was this well that satisfied thirst?

At times I found myself complaining about the weather, too hot, too much rain, too cold, and on and on. I was brought face to face with my sin and told not to say such things because all comes from God. He gives us everything in His perfect time and amount, for He is Master.

Being drawn to the vital faith of the people, I asked them to share with me. Having used a rote meal prayer, I inquired what was said in their silence with bowed heads before eating. They thanked God and praised Him for the bounty brought before them, an expression of their solid rock faith in God Who fed them daily. Often tried by the fires of prejudice and injustice, they evidenced strength steeled by God's Word and His promises. The Mississippi Delta people may have been poor materially, but I discovered that I was the one who was poor spiritually.

Leaving the Convent

During the next thirteen to fourteen years, I struggled with the realization that I was a prisoner, mentally, emotionally and spiritually. I came to realize that I was trying to live up to human expectations. God had a different design for my life.

College opened my eyes to the fact that there were two very different sides to my personality. One played a role and the other was free-spirited. One day in particular while returning to the motherhouse in Tiffin, Ohio, I had a picture come to mind of going back to be caged up again.

When I went apartment hunting after graduation, I began separating from the idea that another authority needed to be making this decision for me. I knew for the first time that I could no longer be obedient to a code of law or to my vow of obedience. Soon after this realization, I told those in charge that I had to leave with no turning back. Finally, at the age of forty-eight, I walked out into the world, as fresh and naive as a teenager.

God led me all the way, confirming after each step of faith I took. The day I moved into the apartment is

"Caged up in convent life"

the day I received Christ as my Savior. Peace like a river flooded over me. There was a freedom in new life that only Christ could offer.

The Meaning of Salvation

Once I told the sisters in my small community, I had a deep sense of loss. With feelings of being stripped bare, I woke crying that night. My tears became tears of relief as God gave me assurance in my decision that I did not need to punish myself any more, trying to make up for my faults and sins. Jesus Christ had fully paid for my sins. Though I did not understand it at the time, He was preparing me for my next step of faith which would involve turning away from my birth faith, Roman Catholicism, and depending on Him alone.

Learning the Word of God

Each time I read the Bible and heard the Word preached, it was as if the Lord opened my ears for the first time to His message. For the first time, I knew God's will for my life and did not need to search for it. Daily Bible reading, from Genesis to Revelation, laid out a complete picture of God's plan for me. By God's grace I was able to comprehend and grow in response to His marvelous message.

I did not have any idea of what was ahead, but God did. After leaving financial and job security, companionship, friends and thirty years of trying to find joy, He did not leave me orphaned. Little did I know then that a seemingly unimportant decision to accept an invitation to go from my apartment complex pool to a ladies' swim party would again change the direction of my life. Here I met a preacher's wife named Millie. She clearly presented from Scripture the work of God in a person who calls upon the name of the Lord.

Having been taught to confess my sins, Roman 3: 10 which says, *"There is none righteous, no, not one"*, was no surprise to me. Nor was I surprised to learn that I deserved death because I was a sinner, *"For the wages of sin is death, but the gift of God is eternal life through Jesus Christ, our Lord"* (Romans 6:23). All my life, the picture of Jesus hanging on the cross had been engraved in my mind, emphasizing the price He paid for my sins. Every Good Friday I had celebrated this event faithfully. Suddenly that picture came alive for me, *"God commendeth his love toward us in that, while we were yet sinners, Christ died for us"* (Romans 5:8).

What I had not known before or heard read in the Scriptures was Romans 10:13, *"For whosoever shall call upon the name of the Lord shall be saved."* I did not know that heaven and eternal life with God was His gift through Jesus Christ. All that was necessary was to believe and accept the truth of the Gospel that Jesus died, was buried, and rose again (Corinthians 15:3-4) and to trust in Jesus alone for my salvation. What joy there was in understanding that I did not need to punish myself anymore! Tears flowed abundantly as I embraced the freedom that only Christ can give.

The Lord Provides

Millie Hobbins, the pastor's wife, became my friend and encourager, answering my many questions, guiding me and patiently putting up with me. Pastor fed me with the Word of God, teaching me that I needed to be daily nourished by the truth of the Scriptures. The church congregation at Lewis Avenue Baptist Church in Temperance, Michigan, helped me through this transitional period. The Lord had provided all that I needed to understand the gift of salvation and begin living as a believer.

My apartment manager, Bessie, had become my friend also. I was very nervous and unsure of myself as it was the first time in my life that I had to make my own choices for things as simple as what kind of toothpaste to buy. No one was telling me what to do or when to do it! Bessie helped me settle into my apartment and she was the one who invited me to the swim party where I met Millie. When she informed me a week later that her car had broken down, making it impossible for her to get to church, I volunteered to take her. Little did I know what that day would bring.

Blessed Assurance

Truth rang like a bell that Sunday in the preaching and teaching. I was convicted to make a public testimony of what Christ had done in my life. The pastor's wife had stopped by my apartment for a visit the day before and planted a seed about baptism. Although I was not really listening then, God used her to prepare me for the next step. In obedience to God's Word, I returned to church that night to publicly profess my faith through believer's baptism.

What a change has come into my life! No longer am I tormented with doubt as to whether or not I am praying right or whether God hears me. From reading the Bible and hearing the preaching of the Word of God, I know how to pray. God's will for my life is also not something about which I worry. I know He wants me to spread the Good News about salvation to everyone I can. I

"I truly praise God for His faithfulness to me."

have learned that forgiveness is necessary for cleansing and to be open to His direction in my life. Stories of how God has worked in the lives of others, especially missionaries, have been a tremendous encouragement.

With God's help and the willingness to be obedient, I can grow in Him and be His disciple. There is excitement in the many truths and promises that are being opened up to me.

I praise God for His faithfulness in dealing with me!

Rita A. Riel

From Religion to Relationship

In September of 1949, I graduated from the eighth grade with an unusual gift—a Bible! It was given to me by Father Charles Moisan, my pastor. He said, "God wrote this book!" I was so very happy to own and cherish the book God wrote.

When I entered the convent at the age of fourteen, I began to read God's Book. I joined the Sisters of Sainte Chretienne, a French order founded in Metz, France, in the early 1800's. At that time, the nuns had an all-girls' high school in Massachusetts. Three groups of students attended the school: the day girls who lived in the area, the boarders, and the juvenists. Juvenist was the name given to a girl aspiring to become a nun. I belonged to this group. There were nineteen newcomers my first year, and all about the same age. Juvenists were isolated and lived under strict convent regulations. Forbidden to speak with anyone outside our group, including even our teachers, we lived mostly in silence. We were only allowed to go home twice a year, two weeks at Christmas vacation and eight weeks during the summer months. As for our families, we could write home once a month and receive their visit once a month. That is all. We made no phone calls home, and our letters were read before we received them. Because of the austere way we lived, many became extremely lonely, including myself.

Why I Wanted to be a Nun

It was unbearable for me to live under these conditions because I missed my family. I was the oldest of five. The youngest had just been born five months earlier, and my mother needed me at home. She had never consented to my leaving in the first place, but I desperately wanted to give my life to God because He had spared mine when I was an infant. Dad told me that Mother prayed to the saints during the four months I was dying in intensive care. The saints in heaven did not do anything for me. When she prayed directly to God, I was healed that day. There were two more reasons why I wanted to be a nun. Since childhood, I had great hopes of being a teacher. The other reason was that I feared death. This one was superior to the other two because I feared that when I died I would go to hell. When the nuns told us about purgatory, it made me feel a little better; but it did not take away the fear. Through being afraid of hell for myself, I began to feel the same fear for my family. I figured that if I could become a nun, I could save my mother, father, sisters and brothers from hell through the disciplinary way of living I was embracing; but I was not sure.

Attempted Escape

After living in the convent for two weeks, I found that I could not go through with this monastic life because it seemed to accentuate the fears even more. While I waited for my parents to come to get me, secretly I packed my belongings. I could not understand what was taking them so long. After all, my mother should have been happy to receive my first letter since I left home two weeks earlier, especially after reading that I wanted her and Dad to come to get me as soon as possible.

I was astonished upon seeing the nun in charge of the juvenists enter the room with my unsealed letter in her hand three days later! The reason I had not sealed it was because we were asked to give it to her so that she could mail it for us. I supposed she wanted to correct my many grammatical mistakes. As she spoke, guilt came into my heart. Was I being disobedient to God? Wasn't this my life to make the choice I wanted to make? Surely, God would not force me to stay in a place against my will. The sister said I was not giving God enough time and that I should stay the full school year to know God's will for my life. "A whole year!", I kept thinking as I looked up at her standing silently beside my desk. I reluctantly nodded, "yes". She then said, "Very well, take this letter and rewrite it. If you let on that you are lonely, your parents will feel badly for you." From that day, I counted the months, days, hours, and finally the minutes. At the end of that time, I still felt the same I had the day I wrote my first letter nine months earlier.

Back Home and Fear

The following year found me happily living at home with the joy I once had. Would it last? While this new school year was in progress, the juvenate nun, the one who persuaded me to stay in the convent, asked me to visit her, which I did. As she conversed with me alone, she repeatedly said that I was definitely opposing God's will by staying home. She also added that God would punish me and my children if I ever got married. Bless her heart! I am sure she did not realize the seriousness of her words, for I received what she said as being true. Now I had an added fear. I was afraid to stay home for fear that if I married, my children would be punished for my disobedience in not becoming a nun. I began to think about my year in the convent. If living my life like this could save my family from spending an eternity in hell, aren't one hundred years of convent life worth it? With this emotional thought tearing me apart, I decided to re-enter the convent at the age of sixteen.

Giving All Yet No Assurance

When I was seventeen, I was never to return home again, not even for a visit, with the exception that when my parents died, I could go for three days. I was sent to their novitiate where, after two years, I would become a full-fledged nun by taking vows. Sorrow filled my heart at the disappointment that no one there had the security of knowing the truth I was seeking concerning eternal life. No one knew for sure if she would go straight to heaven when she died. That was incredible! Why should we live years of deprivation from a normal life if one was not sure? Yet, we were instructed that it was a mortal sin for one to leave after having made final (also known as perpetual) vows. I could have left the convent right then but was bound by the words the sister had said a few years earlier that if I married, my children would be punished.

Personal Times with The Lord

Thank God I had a Bible! I continued to read God's book and found it easy to talk about my problems to Jesus because I saw how compassionate He was with those who came to Him. Jesus was the only One who could understand and give me peace in time of trouble. When I went to Him, I had the answers I needed. He became my best Friend. When I made the vow of obedience, I was not allowed to become a teacher because I had not finished high school. That tore me to pieces. This was the second time I felt deceived in the convent, apart from not knowing for sure if I would go to heaven when I died. "You'll know when you get there," priests would say. What if God would not let me into heaven once I arrived at its gates? That question troubled me more than accepting the life-long task to which I was assigned, that is, to do domestic work instead of becoming a school teacher. From the day I was denied my wish to teach, I made it a habit to bring every problem I faced to Jesus. I would go to chapel, close the door, and with much reverence say, "Jesus, I want to have a word with You." When I did that, I knew that Jesus listened. I was very grateful! That day I knelt at the communion rail and had a heart-to-heart talk with my best Friend. I told Him that all the nuns in the auditorium had a class to teach except me, because I was not qualified. "Jesus," I said after letting a few tears drop on the communion rail, "if You say 'yes', the Superiors would give me a classroom of children to teach."

With The Lord, I Begin to Teach

Two weeks later I was on my way to Maine as a substitute teacher to replace a nun who had taken sick with cancer. When I walked into the classroom the following day with no preparation, I was overwhelmed to see forty-seven second graders. The Superior that sent me there for two months did not tell me I would have that many students! We prayed together for their teacher's recovery. I managed to get through the first day of school, made a quick exit from the building, set my books in the community room of the convent, went directly to chapel, closed the door behind me and said, "Jesus, I need to have a word with You." Jesus knows our needs before we go to Him. However, He delights in hearing the prayer of a person who trusts in Him. "First of all, Jesus, I want to thank You for the class You gave me, but I forgot to tell you something. I forgot to tell you that I do not know how to teach." I knew God smiled and was waiting for me to come to Him. With great joy, I realized that I was to turn my class over to Him, which I did immediately. Unknown to me then was that the direction Jesus gave me was the same as that given to Moses by his father-in-law, Jethro. "You have too many children. Delegate your authority. Make pupil teachers out of your students. Teach them to teach others. I will direct you day by day." When Jesus directed me, I understood Him by His grace through

His Holy Spirit. When I went to school, I would apply what Jesus had taught me. God's teaching results were fantastic!

The Superiors discontinued their search for a qualified teacher and I remained a teacher for years to come. I was awarded a year's scholarship to visit progressive schools in England, Scotland, Switzerland, Canada, and throughout the United States of America. Following that year, I was accepted at the University of Massachusetts and graduated with a Master's Degree in education. I give all the glory to Jesus! As I read the Bible that year, Jesus taught me to trust Him with my class.

Trusting in Him

Most importantly, He prepared me to trust Him with my sins that kept me from knowing for sure I was going to heaven. As time passed, I began to tell Jesus my sins. When I did this, I felt peace within my being, but it was not that way when I told them to a priest. Why? Simply because the priest had no power to forgive sins. That power always belonged to God alone, *"...who can forgive sins but God only?"* (Mark 2:7). Do you know that it is terrifying to read that *"...all have sinned and come short of the glory of God"* (Romans 3:23). That meant everyone needed a Savior because we were all damned! What did our Father do about the fact that we were all heading for hell? *"For God so loved the world, that He gave His only begotten Son, that whosoever believeth in Him should not perish but have everlasting life!"* (John 3:16). That is the answer I was searching to find for years!!! Eternal life is secured for us only in Jesus! We can know now that God will let us into heaven when we die because we believe by God's grace in His Son, Jesus, who paid the price for all our sins on the Cross! I had found the answer!!! To believe in purgatory or any other substitute is to deny the Blood of Jesus! Jesus said, *"and ye shall seek me, and find me when ye shall search for me with all your heart"* (Jeremiah 29:13). When we seek God with all our heart, it is because God's grace is working in us through faith. The result of grace is repentance (a complete turn about) from relying on what we do for salvation to believing we are saved by what Jesus did for us through His suffering, death, and resurrection. Once we respond in faith to receive the free gift of salvation, we can show our gratitude by taking a stand for Him with our lives. *"For as the body without the spirit is dead, so faith without works is dead"* (James 2:26).

Salvation and Its Fruit

Thomas fell to his knees in repentance after doubting Jesus' resurrection and said, *"My Lord, and my God."* One of the thieves on the cross confessed he deserved his punishment, said that Jesus was innocent, called Jesus "Lord", and asked Jesus to remember him in Paradise. Jesus said, *"Today shalt thou be with me in paradise"* (Luke 23:43). Zaccheus came down from the sycamore tree, received Jesus into his house joyfully, and said to Jesus that he would give half his goods to the poor, that if he had taken any thing from any man by false accusation, he would restore it to him four-fold. *"And Jesus said unto him, This day is salvation come to this house"* (Luke 19:9). Mary sang her "Magnificat" to Elizabeth when she was with Child, *"And Mary said, my soul doth magnify the Lord, and my spirit hath rejoiced in God my Savior"* (Luke 1:46-47). Did you read that? How exciting! Mary confessed that she needed a Savior also! This verifies the Word of God that says, *"For all have sinned."* Mary, the mother of Jesus and not of God (since Jesus is both God and man), took a stand for Jesus by saying to Elizabeth that she needed a Savior. Later, she verified it again by telling the servants at the wedding feast at Cana, *"Whatsoever he saith unto you, do it"* (John 2:5). Mary wanted us to obey Jesus. Everything Jesus directs us to do is found in the Bible! Check the Bible to see if what is being told to you by me, your pastor, the evangelist, or anyone else is true or false.

Once I came to realize that my faith was in Jesus alone for my salvation, I needed to renounce all idolatry. Part of idolatry is praying outside of God's order. God's order in prayer is to pray to our Father in Jesus' name (John 14:13-14; 16:26), and He will give you the Holy Spirit. This is the Godhead and the order of the Godhead in prayer. I used to pray to Mary, the saints, the angels, and to the Holy Spirit, but I do not find anyone doing that in the Bible. The Word says that Jesus is the only Mediator between God and man, *"For there is one God, and one mediator between God and men, the man Christ Jesus"* (1 Timothy 2:5). *"...no man cometh unto the Father, but by me"* (John 14:6).

The Spirit of Truth

Although the Holy Spirit is God, He gives preeminence to Jesus (Colossians 1:18). *"He shall teach you all things, and bring all things to your remembrance, whatsoever I have said unto you"* (John 14:26). The Holy Spirit reproves the world of sin, of righteousness, and of judgment (John 16:8), guides us into all truth, does not speak of Himself (v. 13), and glorifies Jesus (v. 14). Jesus always prayed to His Father. It is not recorded in the Bible that anyone prayed outside of God's order, as many do today!

Jesus never sinned nor was He born of Adam with the original sin. He was the Son of God born of a virgin (Luke 1:35). Therefore, He alone could wash away our sins because He had no sin in Him. Therefore, *"Neither is there salvation in any other: for there is none other name under heaven given among men, whereby we must be saved"* (Acts 4:12). When I came to understand, through Jesus' Holy Spirit, that I could never be saved by my works as I thought I could when I entered the convent, I felt so foolish. Who did I think I was to think I could work to be my own Savior? If that could have been true, then why did Jesus come? He would have suffered and died in vain for me. *"I do not frustrate the grace of God: for if righteousness, comes by the law, then Christ is dead in vain"* (Galatians 2:21). *"And if by grace, then no more of works: otherwise grace is no more grace. But if it be of works, then is it no more grace: otherwise work is no more work. And if by grace, then is it no more of works; otherwise grace is no more grace"* (Romans 11:6). *"Therefore by the deeds of the law there shall no flesh be justified in his sight: for by the law is the knowledge of sin"* (Romans 3:20).

The Gospel is Complete and Finished

Jesus came to shed His sinless Blood for the redemption of all mankind, *"In whom we have redemption through his blood, even the forgiveness of sins"* (Colossians 1:14). Read what Saint Peter said, *"For as much as ye know that ye were not redeemed with corruptible things, as silver and gold, from your vain conversation received by tradition from your fathers; But with the precious blood of Christ, as of a lamb without blemish and without spot"* (1 Peter 1:18-19). When Jesus said, *"It is finished"* (John 19:30), He died *"once for all"* (Hebrews 10:10). His bloodless sacrifice need not be repeated on our altars. The denial of Christ here is twofold. First, it is a bloodless sacrifice. The Word of God says, *"And almost all things are by the law purged with blood; and without shedding of blood there is no remission"* (Hebrews 9:22). Second, it is a repetition of the sacrifice of Jesus that was done once for all. The questions we must ask here are: If the original sacrifice of our blessed Lord needs to be repeated, does that not make the death of Jesus insufficient? And didn't our Lord say, *"It is finished"* at His death?

Born Again, Then Fruitful

The day our Father was drawing me to Jesus, I was alone in chapel. No one but God told me what to do, but that does not mean God does not speak to me through people. I had told Jesus I believed in Him and had given Him all my sins, but had never taken a stand for Him. My communion with Him was personal. Jesus needed to make me strong so I could persevere to weather the storms of life with Him. He wanted my whole heart. If I had an unrepentant habit in my life, it would cause me to serve two masters even though I said I loved Jesus. *"No man can serve two masters: for either he will hate the one, and love the other; or else he will hold to the one, and despise the other. Ye cannot serve God and mammon"* (Matthew 6:24).

At times I was scared to be different. I would say that I loved Jesus, but did I? God tested me to find out if I could overcome peer pressure. The rule stated that when we offended a nun, we were supposed to kiss her feet, ask forgiveness, wait for her to say we were forgiven and kiss her feet again before leaving her. I never wanted to offend a nun so that I would never have to do that, but after a nun gave me the cold treatment for a week, I felt impelled to do that to obtain peace between us. God's grace was sufficient. When I was still kneeling on the floor after kissing the nun's feet once, I asked her to tell me what I did so that I would never do it again. She said, "If you are to continue to talk to the other side, you have no part of me." I was puzzled for an instant, but the Spirit of our Lord helped me. As quick as a flash, I understood that she wanted me to stop talking to the nun she hated. Since God wants us to be kind to everyone, I stood up immediately and said, "You are either a Christian or you are not!" I purposed in my heart that I would never disobey God in order to obey any person. Although I refused to bow down to a spirit of hate, I loved her, and prayed for her. That is the day I was born again. First, God saved me by grace through faith, next He helped me show it by action, *"Except a man be born again, he cannot see the kingdom of God"* (John 3:3).

In Fruitfulness Not Counting the Cost

God's grace continued to follow me to give me strength to stand for Him down through the years whether I lost all my friends in the process or not. What a joy to know that with God's help, I was able to take a stand for the King of Kings and the Lord of Lords, and He'll stand by me and support me with that desire I have to live by His grace as long as I live! It was that same day Jesus helped me overcome peer pressure, and gave me a message I will never forget. I went to chapel and cried because I knew in my heart that I had an enemy that would be persecuting me the rest of my life. When I stopped crying, I asked my best Friend, "Is that what it means to take a stand for you, Jesus?"

Once Jesus became the Lord of my life, my spirit went through a radical change. The best way I can describe my new birth from the natural to the spiritual is what happens when a caterpillar changes by metamorphosis into a beautiful butterfly. Far better still, I became a child of God, adopted in His family, and I fell in love with Jesus! My sins were washed away by the blood of Jesus. I became a new creature in Christ, draped in Jesus' righteousness and an heir of eternal salvation. I could pray to our Father in Jesus' name, and He heard me. Many times my prayer was answered with both physical and spiritual healing. As an example, the sick nun that I replaced in school was healed of cancer and is still alive after forty years! When Jesus became my Lord, I was not afraid to disobey man in order to obey God. When I came to God through His grace, Jesus was working in me through His Word, for He is the Word of God (Revelations 19:13), and we developed an intimate relationship of love. Things began to happen in my soul! Jesus' Word is so powerful that He took fear of dying away from me. It was a total deliverance! I have come to death's door twice now and was not afraid! Glory to God!

"For by grace are ye saved through faith; and that not of yourselves: it is the gift of God: Not of works, lest any man should boast" (Ephesians 2:8-9). Works do not save. They are automatic or spontaneous reflections of a pure heart as a result of salvation (Ephesians 2:10; Philippians 2:12; James 2:18, 20) and not a means of obtaining salvation, as non-Christians believe. We are made of spirit, soul, and body. As though salvation from my sins by giving me a new spirit, which is the eternal life, wasn't enough, Jesus did even more. When He shed His blood for me, He also provided for the healing of my body and soul from sin (Isaiah 53:4-5; 2 Peter 2:24; Matthew 8:17; Luke 22:44). Jesus can help me overcome sin if I trust Him. Body in the Bible is referred to as the flesh. The soul is the mind (I think), will (I want), and emotions (I feel) or as the Bible says, *"But the natural man receiveth not the things of the Spirit of God: for they are foolishness unto him: neither can he know them, because they are spiritually discerned"* (1 Corinthians

2:14). At present Jesus is helping me to overcome the flesh through our relationship, so as to think, want and feel after God's will and not my own.

Please Listen

It is a pity that as I was growing up, no one told me that only Jesus can save me. That is why I'm eager to tell you God's truth today. Tomorrow may be too late! I am sincerely praying that everyone in the world would understand the importance of having a relationship with Jesus today because death can come at any minute! The devil wants to snatch us, but he cannot if we believe in Jesus alone to save us! The error that keeps individuals away from Jesus still exists today. People back then, as today, say at funeral Masses that the deceased person is saved by baptism. How can this be? That is works! God's order for salvation is foundational to our eternal destiny: We must first believe the Good News of the Gospel and then be baptized. Baptism is important only if one believes in Christ Jesus first. Baptism is an outward sign of an inward conversion signifying that we died with Christ and will rise with Christ at the resurrection of the dead, but baptism doesn't save. Can a baby believe? A child needs to have understanding, better known to us as the "age of reasoning." So, how can any one be saved as a baby at baptism? The order of God is completely reversed when we say we are saved as a baby.

He Cares for His Sheep

Down through the years, Jesus often reminded me of His Covenant saying He would never leave me nor forsake me. He even delivered me from a number of physical ailments. Tumors were dissolved in me with no hospital help after two doctors said I needed an immediate operation. In Africa, I was prevented from being paralyzed due to a nearly total severing of my Achilles' tendon. His Word healed me when I called to Him, and He delivered me from malaria and death. Weeks later, I nearly lost all my hair due to the high fever of malaria, but Jesus restored every hair after a medical authority said it would never be restored.

Healing by our Great Physician may not be only physical. After being deceived by a con artist and ending up in jail, God miraculously delivered me. When my feet were in the fire after crashing into a telephone pole at fifty miles per hour, Jesus did not take me home because I still had work to do for Him. The whole car went up in flames seconds after two strangers pulled me out of the car window and laid me on the ground. My heroes told me about the fire my feet were in, and one said he saw the fire turn away from my legs. I was not burned. My nylon stockings were not even singed. "Praise the Lord!" My left socket and hip were crushed in many pieces, but again Jesus healed me after an operation where He helped the surgeons screw the bones together onto a metal plate. I walk and run normally! Someone said, "If we never had problems, how would we know Jesus solves them?"

Questions and Answers

To this day, I still continue to question many things, and Jesus gives me the answer in His Word because the Bible is the only truth and foundation by which we are to live. If we love Jesus, we will keep His commandments (John 14:15). Where do we find them? Yes, in His Word. Down through thousands of years, He has preserved His Word totally as He said He would (Psalm 12:7). *"How shall they believe in him of whom they have not heard?"* (Romans 10:14). Do we love Him and believe on Him by reading His Word every day as our necessary food? Will you deny yourself daily (Luke 9:23)?

My Story and Yours

Did you know that you can know Jesus and have that intimate relationship with Him, too? What He did for me He wants to do for you, also. Many of us former nuns are telling you our story of how we got born-again. We are praying for you because Jesus' compassion for you is real. When you arrive at heaven's gates, won't it be wonderful to hear, "Come in, faithful servant?" God wants you to have that assurance before you die, or it will be too late. *" This is the work of God, that ye believe on him whom he hath sent"* (John 6:29) are the words Jesus wants to say to you also, dear reader. He has no favorites. He said that He would draw close to you if you draw close to Him (James 4:8). Will you believe on Jesus alone? Will you forsake all for Him (Matthew 19:29)? He forsook all for you. He said, *"The foxes have holes, and the birds of the air nests; but the Son of man hath not where to lay his head"* (Matthew 8:20).

"We are praying for you"

45

I believe the question God is asking today and has always asked each person down through man's history is, "With whom do you want to be identified? a church? a religion? a culture? an ideology? popular opinion? success? prosperity? or with my Son, the Lord, Jesus Christ?" Take time now to think on what the Lord Jesus did for you at Calvary. He died in your place, for your sin. Think of the eternal rewards He offers as you. Believe on Him alone and follow Him daily in this life. Many may have deceived you in your religion, as they did me, but Jesus never deceived me in all these forty years since the day He opened my eyes and I trusted in His finished sacrifice for me. I'd rather obey Jesus, wouldn't you? We can trust our Lord Jesus because He will never lie to us. If you desire to converse with Jesus, tell Him you love Him and believe in Him. Give Jesus all your sins, and ask Him to be your Lord and Savior. Jesus tells us that He is the only way to the Father. *"I am the Way, the Truth, and the Life. No man cometh to the Father but by me"* (John 14:6). I repeat, Jesus is the only Mediator between God and man (1 Timothy 2:5). May Jesus have the preeminence in your life always, and you will be honoring our Father in heaven (Colossians 1:18-19)! In His graciousness believe on Him, *"To the praise of the glory of His grace, wherein He hath made us accepted in the Beloved"* (Ephesians 1:6).

Mary C. Hertel
(formerly Sister Mary Dolora, C.S.J.)

The Unsearchable Ways of God

"If therefore the Son shall make you free, you shall be free indeed."
John 8:36

Having taken the vows of poverty, chastity and obedience in a Roman Catholic diocesan order, my steps were set in the logical direction prepared by my youth. Raised in a strong Catholic home, educated in Catholic schools for sixteen years, and trained by six years of convent life, I lived with an eagerness to serve God as a teacher. This desire did not change when I left the convent in 1969. Two years later, I married a man whose background was strikingly similar, including four years in the seminary and a commitment to teaching. Yet, despite these roots, God's unsearchable ways set me on a new path which brought me face to face with truth in the Person of His Son, Jesus Christ.

Early Years

While God's ways are a mystery to me, His grace is unmistakable as I reflect back on my life at age fifty in the year 1995. The third in a family of four, I shared a relatively stable home environment around the alcoholism of my father. My mother worried continuously, particularly about finances and my father's condition between the two to three jobs he worked. Mass and Communion, rosaries, novenas and other special devotions to Mary, the Sacred Heart, the Infant of Prague, St. Joseph, St. Anthony, St. Christopher and others were rituals of our daily life. When our family home was honored by our parish with the rotating statue of Mary, daily rosary on our knees and other devotional prayers were intensified. My mother took church rules seriously. Fasting and abstinence for Advent and Lent and meatless Fridays were carefully observed. The fat of bacon or gravy from meat was scrupulously avoided in meal preparation during these times. Obtaining indulgences and purchasing Masses for the deceased was performed as a means of shortening time in purgatory. There was a heaviness in our home, yet there was a stability regarding the life-long commitment of marriage, attendance at church and association with only Catholics as friends and even acquaintances. The few extended family members that violated these patterns were rarely seen, spoken of infrequently, and their marriage ceremonies were not attended.

Religious Life

Until I was in my twenties, I was never inside a non-Roman Catholic Church. Religious and priests were held in high esteem, thought to be both holier and wiser than the laity. A cousin, Vin, entered the Marianist brotherhood at age 15, a decision held above the strong marriage relationships in our family. Vin influenced his two younger sisters, Sue and Peg, who later entered the Ursuline convent. Two years after Vin's youngest sister entered the convent, I made the same decision, to the delight of my family. The diocesan order known as the Congregation of Sisters of St. Joseph, which had taught me all through elementary and high school, would enable me to fulfill my dream of going to college and of becoming a teacher.

This decision to become a religious was supported especially by my mother. It was a matter of pride and honor for the family. At

the time I entered in 1963, the rule was that I would never return home. As a postulant, communication with family was monitored (letters written home and received from home were read) and strict rules were in place for the years of training. After the first year, a bridal ceremony followed by the cutting of

"First year as a postulant, visiting with my family"

my hair and dressing in full restrictive habit ushered me into the Novitiate. I was now Sister Mary Dolora. I spent a year away from college for serious formation.

During this year, I was indoctrinated in the proper manner of thought, speech and behavior for a professed religious. Silence, limitations on with whom I could talk and when, and not being able to attend my sister Carol's wedding began to raise questions regarding the purpose of such restrictions. Learning obedience involved such practices as falling on one's knees to ask for penance when there was an infraction of the rules. On one occasion, I personally struggled when this humiliating practice was imposed on me because I had talked to a lonely older sister during infirmary duty.

"In the Novitiate in full habit, with my parents"

By the end of the third year, massive change was sweeping the Roman Catholic Church and some of it reached our small diocesan order. The year before my class was to begin self-flagellation as a means to higher spirituality, the practice was discontinued. By my second year in the novitiate, even my class was vested with the surprising responsibility of designing a much less confining habit. Rules were examined at a special congregation meeting of all the superiors. Soon, the hated ban on visiting home was lifted.

Arbitrary Change

With all of the change, questions about the significance of arbitrary rules began to concern me. How could these rules be so important

"The new, less restrictive habit"

one day and dismissed the next? There were abuses during the changes that reimposed some disciplines and older sisters in authority saw major problems developing. An example occurred during my first full year of teaching at a parish assignment. Word of "friendly" parties involving priests and nuns, which included dancing and frivolity, got back to the motherhouse and our local parish convent was verbally chastised and watched.

In addition, permission I had been given to visit a wonderful family in the parish was withdrawn. I found this particularly troubling since the wife had grown up on my street and her husband, George, had multiple sclerosis that paralyzed him from the neck down. I was able to share many things with them and their three children, most importantly, a listening ear, laughter and tears. The witness of love in this family left a great impression on me. Being unable to visit made no sense. Later that same year, when one of my sixth grade students, Jeff, sustained a serious head injury, only plaintive pleas from his mother enabled me to tutor him in the hospital during his long recovery. At no time was there any clear basis for the arbitrary rule changes, only a fear of serious infractions. It was God's grace that enabled me to learn and move on from the situations with George and Jeff. Rules intended to produce holiness through behavior control were shallow in the face of real life challenges.

A Leave of Absence

In 1969, near the end of my first full year in a parish teaching assignment, I seriously considered a leave of absence from religious life. Prior to this year, leaving the convent after taking vows would have meant failure or disgrace. However, now the request to take a year to evaluate one's vocation was acceptable. While I was not the only one thinking this way, I was the first from my class of nine to solicit a meeting with the Mother Superior.

I know my family was disappointed, but I did not focus on their approval. Instead, I determined to move forward from the confinement of convent life to an environment that would foster personal query. It was June of 1969. I had only the clothes on my back and a small savings from high school employment that my parents kept in my name. After two weeks at home, I attended Ohio State University with another convent sister and then took a teaching position in Chicago, moving into a large inner city home with a civil rights leader, Margaret Ellen Traxler, also a nun. I shared a room with a classmate from the convent and we lived in the home with other nuns who worked with Margaret Ellen. After a sheltered convent life, that summer of '69 and the year that followed opened my eyes to all the "flavor" of the late sixties—war protests, racial tensions, alcohol, drugs, free sex, undisciplined hours, discussions of Eastern mystical philosophies—in a volatile large city. Moral standards learned in my home and the grace of God, which I didn't recognize until much later, protected me both physically and spiritually. Many around me from similar backgrounds were choosing self-destructive life styles.

After seven months, I moved to an apartment near the University of Chicago. At the Newman Center, I met many former nuns and priests, some leaving their orders in larger numbers, some remaining but studying primarily various interpretations of "truth". Mass and communion were performed around coffee tables, the social gospel was prevalent, civil rights was a banner. People who were clear about what they believed and where they were going were not to be found. Causes were in, morality was out. Through all of this, I knew I would never return to the convent. I made the final break from my vows and order.

Marriage

When I recall the situations I was in during these years in Chicago, I marvel at God's hand of protection. His care for me included living in Hyde Park, a racially mixed community during a time of much racial tension, and University of Chicago parties where free sex, drugs, bazaar thinking with drugged or duped minds, and generally loose living abounded. After dating a number of relatively stable men in such an environment, I met my husband, Bernie, an ex-seminarian. It was early in 1970 and I was twenty-five. With comparable backgrounds giving us much in common, we dated only a few weeks before talking of marriage. However, we took a full year to become acquainted with our families in Ohio and Wisconsin and to lay careful plans for our wedding.

For our marriage ceremony, we choose the church where I taught my last year in the convent rather than my family parish. My Superior from that assignment was there as well as George's widow and others I knew from my teaching. Both Bernie and I were very family oriented and decided to settle in Michigan, within a day's drive of our parents. Here we began our family and lived as active members of St. Peter's Parish for five and one half years.

Times of Testing

Our two children were ages two and four months when my mother was diagnosed with an inoperable brain tumor. Frequent travel from Michigan to Ohio during her rapid decline required many arrangements and a doubling of duties for my husband. She died less than six months after being diagnosed. A year later, I was six weeks pregnant with our third child when I received a call from my sister. She had found my father dead in bed. He failed to show up for dinner at her home. Throughout this difficult time, Bernie was the Lord's provision of support.

Six months after my father's death, we moved to the Milwaukee area. During the following six months, Bernie's mother had open heart surgery during which she experienced a partially disabling stroke, our third daughter was born, and Bernie went through two difficult job changes. It seemed as though our lives were in constant upheaval. Among my part-time jobs was a position as religious education director for a large parish in our suburban community. It was here that I was introduced to values clarification, a move away from the clear moral traditions and doctrines of Roman Catholicism, and the diminished use of the sacrament of confession. These practices and an introduction to increasingly liberal teachings of men like Daniel Maguire of Marquette University and Archbishop Rembert Weakland produced growing confusion.

In some cases I seriously questioned these new trends and in other cases I accepted them as a positive new direction. It was "in" to be a part of the new ideas. All three of our daughters were baptized, made their first communion and were taught reconciliation (formerly the sacrament of confession), although it was not practiced at our parish. During the eleven years we were at this parish, I taught and wrote curriculum for CCD classes and/or directed religious education programs.

Uprooting

The last year and a half, Bernie and I taught high school confirmation classes together in our home. Ironically, God used this program and the man who directed it to complete the groundwork that would dislodge our deep roots in Roman Catholicism. When the director gave us and our students each a Catholic Bible, he could not have known that he had provided not simply a resource but a vehicle of liberation. This was the beginning of our study of the Word of God.

The Confirmation textbook given with the Bible presented not doctrine, but the social gospel—a system of works that were to be the sanctifying process for the "Christian". Homilies were no better. Talks with our pastor about concerns went nowhere. Serious moral situations that surfaced in discussions with our students made it clear there was no spiritual foundation for decision-making. Again by God's grace, we were directed to turn to the Bible. A growing discomfort with what appeared to be a course headed for destruction fostered a desire in me for a much more conservative position. Strong family values and the moral foundation we hoped to pass on to our students as well as our daughters was no longer sustained by our parish church.

Our oldest daughter, Laura, was in confirmation classes this same year with another couple. She, too, was experiencing great difficulty with the material, particularly the way students ignored more traditional moral positions. At the same time, the public schools where all three of our daughters attended, proposed liberal sex education curriculums. Concern about this material introduced me to a whole new set of friends who were confident in their beliefs and what they wanted for their children. Lowering standards to "fit the times" was not in their thinking. Working with this group of people in a difficult fight for the welfare of our children brought Bernie and me into more and more contact with the Word of God.

Unchangeable Truth

We were invited to join Bible studies and prayer groups and Bernie and I became convicted of the authority of the Word of God. Bernie proposed lessons based on the Bible and the Nicene Creed for our confirmation group and they were approved by the director. We offered Bible-based curriculum to replace muddled thinking and fruitless discussions with God's unchangeable principles. When questions arose that we could not deal with, we found experts through our new Christian friends. One spoke on the authority of the Word of God and one addressed issues regarding the occult and Satanism. These were not priests or religious but lay persons who knew and stood on the truth of Scripture.

Although I cannot point to one specific day that I recognized and accepted Jesus Christ as my Savior, the truth of His Word was taking root in my life by the summer of 1989. In June, abiding by the sound advice of the man who would be our first local church pastor, *"wives be in subjection to your own husbands that, if any obey not the word, they also may without the word be won by the behavior of their wives"* (1Peter 3:1), I asked Bernie's permission to attend worship service at a Bible-based church. He said yes!

Conviction

Our daughters were fifteen, thirteen, and eleven at the time. I knew there would be questions and I worried about the affect on our family unity. We attended both Catholic and Christian churches for most of the summer. Bernie tried the Christian church at my request for my birthday in July. His permission for me and agreement to attend with me were clear indications that God was involved in the circumstances of our lives.

Another dramatic example was a Sunday early in the summer when I suddenly could not receive communion at a Catholic Mass. The stark realization that I did not believe this could be the "real" body and blood as taught by the Catholic Church was a startling and profound faith conviction. To have gone forward would have been hypocrisy. I realized that eating the body and blood according to the Bible meant much more, an identification with the Person of Jesus Christ. It did not make sense that He would be present in me at communion and not there the rest of the time. There was no magic or mystery. The words of the priest said to have the power of transforming bread and wine were a denial of the sufficiency of the work of the cross. Jesus said, *"It is finished"* (John 19:30). Communion is a memorial of what He has accomplished. His command was to *"Do this in remembrance of Me"* (Luke 22: 19).

The Mass prayers also stuck in my throat. Why was sacrifice still necessary? *"He is able also to save them to the uttermost that come unto God by Him, seeing He ever liveth to make intercession for them"*; He *"needeth not daily ... to offer up sacrifice ... for this He did once for all when He offered up Himself "* (Hebrews 7: 25 & 27). The "unbloody sacrifice", as the Mass was defined, contradicted what both the Old and New Covenant taught, *"without shedding of blood there is no forgiveness"* (Hebrews 9: 22). He had *"offered one sacrifice for sins for all time"* and *"by the one offering has perfected those who are sanctified"* (Hebrews 12 & 14). The veil of the Holy of Holies has been torn in two. Man has access to the throne of God.

The revelation regarding communion initiated one of many lively spiritual discussions in our family during this time. This was completely out of the ordinary, yet I know now that the power of the Word of God was effecting a spiritual revolution in our lives regarding the Roman Catholic teaching concerning the Person and the power of the Lord Jesus Christ.

By August we were no longer attending Mass, which we saw as a denial of the finished work of Calvary. We missed the liturgical rituals, weekly participation in communion, and familiar contacts. Neither extended family nor Catholic friends understood what we were doing; yet we were convicted. Much to our surprise, when we told the religious education director at our now former parish, he asked us to continue teaching our confirmation group through their second year because "good teachers were hard to find" and our class had been positively responsive.

At Christmas we wrote a letter to our relatives and friends regarding our conversion. This initiated distress, anger and painful distancing. The significance of Matthew 19:29 which had been quoted so many times in relation to religious life suddenly became clear: "*And every one that hath forsaken houses, or brethren, or sisters, or father, or mother, or wife, or children, or lands, for my sake, shall receive an hundredfold, and shall inherit everlasting life.*"

In my own inadequacy to put into words what it meant to be saved, I invited a Christian woman over to explain salvation to our daughters. It was our youngest, Allison's, first exposure to the Gospel. Our oldest, Laura, showed me a journal entry she had made recording the day she accepted Jesus Christ as her salvation more than a year earlier. She had a circle of Christian friends at school and was regularly studying the Bible. Our second daughter, Sarah, later shared that she had first heard the Gospel at a summer camp two years before. Although she believed what Jesus had done for her, there was little impact in her life because she had no training in the Word of God when camp was over.

Conversion

God's intervention leading the five of us out of Roman Catholicism is nothing short of a miracle, the miracle of conversion in the life of every believer. I have since realized that the more than forty years I spent in the Catholic Church, faithfully attending rituals and going through extensive religious training, did not bring me to a knowledge of the Gospel. I was a sinner hopelessly lost without God's perfect provision. "*Christ died for our sins according to the scriptures;... was buried, and...rose again the third day according to the Scriptures*" (1Corinthians 15:3-4). This and this alone saved me. Nothing can be added to the work of Jesus Christ nor can His work be re-enacted to bring forgiveness and grace. God prepared and drew us to Himself through His Word, the Bible, not through religious traditions and institutions.

Believer's Baptism

Our family's continued spiritual transformation brought us to seek baptism by immersion in May of 1993. Knowing that baptism is not efficacious (i.e., it does not wash away sin and establish relationship with God, as taught by Catholicism), we initially did not think it necessary to be baptized. The first Christian church we attended baptized infants in the context of the a "covenant family relationship". We questioned this practice because it was not directed by Scripture. In 1993, Bernie and I met a pastor from North Carolina who showed us from Scripture that baptism was an important public witness and a matter of obedience. Again, the Lord was teaching us apart from a local church, establishing for us the authority of His Word. We were *"to examine the Scriptures daily"*, using the Word of God as the authority in our lives (Acts 17:11). After presenting what we had learned to our daughters, we discovered that our oldest, Laura, who was at college in Pennsylvania, desired to be baptized and was praying about it since her mission trip the previous summer. Our younger daughters, Sarah and Allison, after study and prayer also sought baptism. We prepared as a family, writing our first testimonies for the ceremony. Our family agreed that baptism was an important public confirmation of our conversion and call by the Lord.

The Walk of Faith

And our story continues until the Lord calls us home. God's impact in my life and on our family stems from our commitment to prayer, study of the Word, fellowship as believers, and our response to His daily direction in our lives. However, the issue of eternal salvation is settled. There is peace, hope and joy in this certainty. The times of loneliness and estrangement after leaving the Catholic Church have diminished with time, but are not gone, especially because our extended families are still Catholic. Knowing the truth, we long for salvation for those we love. Sharing with relatives and others is often sadly devoid of eternal perspective.

After we left our first Christian church, we again went through a period of wilderness, disappointment in relationships and concern for differences of scriptural interpretation and application among believers. However, the Lord never left us without His peace. Answers were available. We understood that membership in the true church was only possible by rebirth (John 3:5). Finding a local church where we could be equipped to serve the Lord would be accomplished in God's time as we found a pastor committed to preaching the entire counsel of the Scriptures. The Bible was given by God to be read and understood, hindered only by our laziness or unwillingness to allow the Holy Spirit to teach us all things (John 14:26). Believers and pastors were put into our lives to encourage and support us, and when they were removed Christ was always sufficient.

Distinguishing between the Word of God and the traditions of men has become a way of life. Recognizing that the standards of God do not change with the times and that His truth is completely trustworthy did not alleviate the challenges of our time. But it provided stability, direction and hope. Jesus Christ is God's Word and the Word is Truth. If I do not live the victorious life of a Christian, it is because of my failure to live drawing upon the resources continually available to me in Christ.

In Summary

The testimony of any Christian is the finished work of Jesus in His death, burial and resurrection accepted by faith as the only thing necessary for salvation. Each story, however, is as unique as the individual because it is always God reaching out to the individual, exactly where each one is. I am grateful for the deep roots of Roman Catholicism in my life, for my parents who gave me physical life and the home and training that laid a strong moral foundation. However, it is God in His infinite wisdom Who *"causes all things to work together for good to those who love God, to those who are called according to His purpose"* (Romans 8:28). And His purpose is to choose, to call, to justify and to sanctify—to conform to the image of His Son (Romans 8:29-30). I marvel at the ways of our God who could transform the first forty-four years of my life as a Roman Catholic, releasing me from the bondage of a religious system steeped in the traditions of men, and bringing me into the freedom of relationship with Jesus Christ. It can only be summarized simply by God's amazing grace, for by grace His servant was saved through faith; and that not of myself, it is the gift of God; not a result of works, that no one should boast. For I am

His workmanship, created in Christ Jesus for good works, which God prepared beforehand, that I should walk in them (Ephesians 2:8-10).

An Addendum

Two years have passed since the writing of this testimony. God's faithfulness and the need for diligence in living according the Word of Truth are the on-going theme of life in relationship with Jesus Christ. Being saved from the penalty of sin the moment one believes and being accepted by the Father in Christ with His perfect righteousness, does not remove the daily struggle to walk in the Spirit so as not to fulfill the desires of the flesh (Galatians 5:16). In times of temptation, trial, and testing, the Holy Spirit will bring to remembrance Scripture we have studied. God's grace and completely adequate provision in every circumstance enables us by the power of the Spirit to live according to His commands and grow in holiness. His grace is always sufficient as He directs what is impossible apart from Him: "*Study to show thyself approved unto God, a workman that needeth not to be ashamed, rightly dividing the word of truth*" (2 Timothy 2:15).

"My husband Bernie."

Personal study of the Word continues to be a part of the lives of each family member. It is a blessing of unity and strength as challenges increase. Our daughters are now twenty-four, twenty-two, and nineteen. They have stability because of God's unchangeable truth while so much in society seems to be lost in a futility of self-focus and "anything goes".

My husband, Bernie, is the spiritual head of our home, seeking to direct us in wisdom gained from biblical knowledge. He conducts a men's Bible study weekly and coordinates monthly Bible study weekends with pastor-teachers, an outreach ministry of Duluth Bible Church. Daily decisions are made more and more in light of a growing understanding of God's purposes and the need for a believer to do all for His glory.

In my own life, I have been learning the role of the woman in the home, being a helpmate to her husband, providing a place of

"Our three daughters and me"

hospitality and times of fellowship with believers as well as opportunities to share with unbelievers. Even as our children have become adults, employment outside the home has a clear second place to the noble role that God intended for woman.

As I have grown in a knowledge of the Word of God, opportunities to disciple others and more recently participate in the Berean Beacon Ministry to Roman Catholics have been special blessings. There is balance in life as a believer that reflects joy, peace, and fruitfulness, the "natural" result of living according to God's purposes.

Knowing God's will and living according to it is a daily challenge. Being faithful is dependent on continual trust in His way, *"Trust in the Lord with all thine heart, and lean not unto thine own understanding. In all thy ways acknowledge him, and he shall direct thy paths"* (Proverbs 3: 5-6). While my family and I have grown, times of failing are just as clear. Failure and sinful choices are very much a part of our lives. God's provision is confession that will immediately put us back in the joy of His fellowship, ready to begin again. *"If we confess our sins, He is faithful and just to forgive us our sins, and to cleanse us from all unrighteousness"* (1 John 1:9).

It is my prayer that all who read this testimony will be drawn to a knowledge of Jesus Christ. He is the Truth that sets every person free to live life abundantly here on earth and for all eternity (John 10: 10). *"Not that we are sufficient of ourselves...but our sufficiency is of God...*

And God is able to make all grace abound toward you, that ye, always having all sufficiency in all things, may abound to every good work" (2 Corinthians 3:5 and 9:8).

"Now unto Him that is able to keep you from falling, and to present you faultless before the presence of His glory with exceeding joy, to the only wise God, our Savior, be glory and majesty, dominion and power, both now and forever. Amen" (Jude 24-25).

Mary Ann Pakiz

God's Word Needs No Authority Other Than Itself

God's Word needs no authority other than itself. When I comprehended that principle, I was free—free to search the Scriptures for truth! In them, I found the way to God. Man gets to God God's way, through Jesus Christ, as revealed in the Bible. *"I am the way, the truth, and the life; no man cometh unto the Father but by me"* (John 14:6).

The Authority Issue

For many years, I had been led to believe that the Catholic Church was the final authority of my faith, and that I had no right to question its teaching. The Roman Catholic system teaches that all authority comes from God, but that God has appointed the Catholic system to be the guardian of His authority. Therefore, everything has to be weighed in the light of Catholic tradition and teaching, as theirs is held to be the only system in which truth is deposited. A Catholic cannot believe in the Scriptures without the authority of the Church to accredit the Scriptures! The Roman Catholic Church declares that God's authority is not sufficient to oblige men to believe and bow to it; it seeks to place church authority above God's authority. **True faith is faith in what God has said because God has said it!** Faith in God is belief in God's Word, the Bible, without any authority other than itself. *"Thou shalt worship the Lord thy God, and Him only shalt thou serve"* (Luke 4:8).

Catholic Baptism

I came under Catholic authority in 1948 when I was re-baptized and converted to Catholicism. I was born in 1930 to Finnish immigrant parents of a Lutheran persuasion. Our neighbors, who were immigrants from Yugoslavia and Italy, had a strong influence on my formative years. As exemplary Catholics, who witnessed to us about their faith and who lived lives of good works and good deeds, of which we often were the recipients, they were committed to bringing the neighborhood under the headship of Rome. They reached out to us with what they thought was the truth. They were sincere, but sincerely wrong. It is important to remember that individual Catholics are not our enemies; rather, they are precious souls who God loves and who He commands us to reach with the Gospel of His Grace. Salvation is by grace. Grace is unmerited favor. We cannot earn grace, nor do we deserve grace. *"For by grace are ye saved through faith; and that not of yourselves, it is the gift of God: Not of works, lest any man should boast"* (Ephesians 2:8-9).

Faith's Object

The Roman Catholic believes that salvation is based on water and works. Baptismal regeneration is the cornerstone of the Catholic system. The Church teaches that no one can enter the kingdom of heaven unless he or she is baptized. The source of Catholic faith is the Church. Its object is loyalty to the Church. Therefore, Catholic faith is in itself. The Christian, however, knows that salvation is based on Christ's work alone, a finished work to which nothing can be added. The source of Christian faith is the Bible. Its object is Jesus Christ. Therefore, true faith is in a Person. In order for faith to be operative, it must be anchored to the person of Jesus Christ.

Blind Acceptance

Rather than searching the Scriptures for truth to find out if Catholic teaching was in line with God's Word, I blindly accepted everything the priest told me during my instructions to become a Catholic, except for one request. He asked me to bring my King James version of the Bible to the rectory. He said it had to be burned because it was not the official Catholic version. Instead, I gave it to my mother.

During my instructions, the stress was on papal supremacy and infallibility. I was told that Christ made Peter the first pope to head the Church on earth with infallible authority. The Pope, as Christ's representative on earth, guided all people, Catholic or not, into all truth (Vatican Council I, 1870). Presently, as I reflect on this Church tenet, I do not find any evidence from Scripture that Christ actually gave any such authority to Peter or even that the apostles considered Peter to have a special position of authority. Furthermore, Peter would have known that he was a pope and certainly would have said something about it. If he had known it, how is it that he did not act as pope?

Becoming a "Bride of Christ"

In 1950, I took another step to come further under Catholic authority by entering the Order of St. Benedict to become a sister. I had been working as a nurse's aide at a local hospital run by the Benedictine Sisters, and, as I was so impressed with their gracious service to the patients and staff, I decided that I, too, wanted to spend my life serving others.

My first year in the convent, as a postulant, was one of the happiest years of my life. Our postulant mistress was a kind, fair, and understanding woman. There were eighteen girls of various ages and backgrounds in our group. They were eager and excited to serve the Catholic Church and to live by the rule of St. Benedict. We shared many happy times together. There were more serious moments for me, too, when I prayed in the chapel and gazed up at the crucifix wondering why Jesus had to die on Calvary's Cross.

Before we became novices, we marched down the church aisle in bridal attire to become "brides of Christ". Nothing much was said about Jesus as we prepared for this event. Rather, our emotions were at high pitch over the changes in our names. I went from Miss

"We were eager to serve. I am on the extreme right"

Mary Ann to Sr. M. Laurian, O.S.B. I was a bride of Christ, and I knew little about Him other than He was the Son of God.

A Stockpile of Good Works

During the five year preparation period for our final vows, we studied the Rule of Saint Benedict, canon law, church history, a bit about Jesuit causistry (the end justifies the means), and the lives of the saints. The emphasis was on self-denial and submission of one's will to the authority figure under whose charge we were. St. Therese, the Little Flower, was held up before us as a role model so we would emulate her way to God. It was a way based on "offering up" the daily vexations of life to make up for our sins or the sins of others. We were busy trying to build a stockpile of good works by which we could make ourselves more acceptable to God. We were offering our self-made sacrifices to God because we did not know that we could get to God because of the offering Jesus Christ had made of Himself in our behalf at Calvary. When Jesus said to God, *"I have finished the work which thou gavest me to do,"* He meant the work He did in behalf of sinners was complete and nothing could be added to it (John 17:4).

Back in the World

In our last three years as scholastics, some of the group left the motherhouse for teaching assignments in the diocese. We returned in the summer, and it was great to be back together again. I needed the rest and relaxation after my first year of teaching forty-five students in grades five and six combined. I had no training in elementary education but was told there would be a blessing in obedience. In 1955, five months before my final vows, I left the convent due to health problems and returned to the home of my parents.

"With my husband"

Back in the world, I was able to get on with my life, by completing my education at the University of Minnesota, earning a Bachelor of Science Degree in Elementary Education, and in 1957, married a man from a staunch Catholic family. We were blessed with two children. My husband's brother is a priest in our diocese, a humble, sweet man who writes poetry about nature, God, and his church.

Salvation's Meaning Brought Home

In 1972, my children, then ages twelve and five, were invited to a neighborhood backyard Bible club. We asked our priest-uncle if they could attend; he didn't seem to be concerned about it and gave his consent. This had to be the work of God! From that point on, our lives were dramatically changed!

The children came home each day with Bible verses to memorize. When they recited them, God touched my heart as well as theirs. I learned the most important truth about myself—**I was a sinner**, and, as such, **was separated from God**! Because God permits no sin or sinner in heaven, I was lost! How was I going to solve this sin issue? I wanted **to be sure** I would go to heaven when I died. I decided to study the Bible on my own. John 17:17, in which Jesus said to God, "*Sanctify them through thy truth; thy word is truth*", was the first verse the Holy Spirit used to undergird my study of salvation.

My search for answers began in Acts 16:31, "*Believe on the Lord Jesus Christ, and thou shalt be saved*", and Acts 4:12, "*Neither is there salvation in any other; for there is no other name under heaven given among men, whereby we must be saved.*" Moving on to Romans, I learned that Christ satisfied the just demands of a Holy God for judgment on sin by His death on the cross. "*Therefore, we conclude that a man is justified by faith apart from the deeds of the law*" (Romans 3:28).

It was an overwhelming realization that none of my past sins had ever been dealt with, even though I had confessed them to the priest and performed the prescribed penance! Going to confession had given me a counterfeit peace and security that my sins had been forgiven by the words of the priest plus the doing of penance. Actually, the priest does not have the power to forgive sins even if he claims he does so in the name of Jesus. Our sins are forgiven only by appropriating the shed blood of Jesus in our place. "*For all have sinned, and come short of the glory of God. Being justified freely by His grace through the redemption that is in Christ Jesus, Whom God hath set forth to be a propitiation through faith in His blood, to declare His righteousness for the remission of sins that are past, through the forbearance of God*" (Romans 3:23-25). God has never given authority to any person to make the decision as to whether another person's sins will be forgiven or not, as He is the only one who truly knows what is in that person's heart. My search caused me to be able to answer the question I asked of myself while in the convent as to why Jesus had to die on the Cross. **Jesus paid the price for my sin by His death on the Cross**! Jesus paid our hell-death penalty in full. Yes, we deserve hell for our sins. Remember, under no circumstance, will God allow sin or a sinner in His heaven. Jesus paid the penalty for our sin so we can spend eternity with God in heaven. The time had come for me to make a decision. Acting on the Bible, as my sole, absolute, and final authority of faith, I received Christ as my Savior in May of 1973. I wanted to shout from the roof tops so all the world could hear what Jesus has done for them by His substitutionary atonement and shed blood. *"And ye shall know the truth, and the truth shall make you free"* (John 8:32).

True Christian Faith and the Roman System

As I witnessed to my Catholic friends and relatives, I saw more clearly that the eternal destiny of many souls was at stake here. I was grieved by their response to the Gospel; they continued to believe that the Catholic Church was the one true church and they trusted it for salvation regardless of what the Bible said. In other words, they had been brought up allowing other human beings or a set of man-made rules to do their thinking for them. In 1545, the Council of Trent declared that church tradition was of equal authority with the Bible. To put anything on a par with or above God's Word is idolatry! In fact, the "leaven" of the Catholic system is the discrediting of the Bible as the sole, absolute, and final authority of faith.

We must think of God rightfully as He is revealed to us through His Word. God the Father and God the Son are one. In John 10:30, Jesus said, *"I and my Father are one."* Because Jesus Christ is God, our sins have been cleansed in the blood of God; only the perfect blood of God could wash them completely away in order to thus satisfy the demands of a holy and righteous God. The ground of my salvation or the basis of my justification is the perfect righteousness of Jesus Christ. When I, by faith, receive (appropriate) the substitutionary atonement of Jesus in my place as full payment of my hell-death penalty, God imputes the righteousness of Jesus Christ to me, that is, He reckons me as righteous. In no way am I righteous of myself, and as such in no way can I save myself or keep myself saved; **it is all of Jesus!** Jesus Christ is my righteousness. It is only "in Christ" that I am righteous. I am not worthy to approach God of myself. However, when I approach God in my substitute, that is, in Christ, I am accounted worthy to do so by God because He sees me in the perfect righteousness of His Son! Justification of the believer is instantaneous.

The Catholic system denies that we are justified by that faith which receives and rests on Christ alone for salvation which is freely offered to us by grace. Instead, they teach we are justified, not simply by faith in Christ, but by faith which has become activated by good works. This faith, as taught in the Catholic system, is said to justify the sinner, not because it rests on the righteousness of Christ, but because it is a righteousness inherent in man, a righteousness which is the product of baptism which makes an individual capable of obedience to the teaching of the Catholic system of divine grace through the sacraments. Justification is not of faith, but of the sacraments. So, therefore, the justification of the Catholic individual is progressive, being regenerated by baptism, being purified from time to time by confession and penance, growing in grace and holiness through the reception of the other sacraments, so that one day he or she will be holy enough to make it to purgatory! So, then, the Catholic believes he is accepted by God by his inherent righteousness which has been sacramentally infused at baptism and nourished by the worthy reception of the other sacraments. As the Catholic receives sanctifying grace attached to each sacrament, he or she is taught that he or she actually becomes righteous or holy on the basis of his own intrinsic worth without any righteousness imputed.

My Mission Field

The differences between the true Christian faith and the Roman Catholic system were becoming so obvious to me that in 1976, I left the Catholic Church and took my place with Bible-believing Christians. When I was saved in 1973, I told the Lord that I would be willing to go to the mission field anywhere. He took me at my word, and, in 1994, sent me to my mission field—dialysis. He permitted my kidney to fail first, and in order to survive, I need dialysis therapy three times a week. I thank and praise God in these circumstances as He has given me the opportunity to share His precious Gospel of Grace with seriously ill patients who need to prepare to meet God!

Jo Ellen Kaminski

His Banner Over Me Is Love

*"He who hears My word...has passed out
of death into life."* (John 5:24)

At age nineteen, I was baptized a Roman Catholic. I had been searching for God and thought I had found the true religion in Catholicism. My new faith was a great comfort to me, but in a few years I began to experience spiritual problems. I yearned for assurance of salvation, but peace eluded me.

I could not even be certain of purgatory! However, I hoped that by my "good works" God would credit my "spiritual bookkeeping", freeing me from that abode entirely. The thought of purgatory terrified me.

"As a young woman"

Fear and Uncertainty

One morning after Mass as I was standing by the "purgatorial altar", in my mind I could hear dimly echoing pleas of her long-dead inhabitants— saved, but doomed to suffer. Out of the caverns of death they seemed to call. It troubled me that the Church taught that God would not help them, but strangely, I could help them by prayers and Masses. Since a money donation was required for Masses, I just prayed. It seemed so out of balance. I left the church that morning uneasy and puzzled.

Each confession was a minor traumatic experience, but the Church said it was God's "sacrament of forgiveness". Without it, sins could not be forgiven. Salvation certainly seemed a "tipsy" affair and God seemed impossible to please; consequently, I turned to Mary and the saints for intercessory prayer, hoping they would slip me through the keyhole if God shut the door.

After about five years of this fear and uncertainty, I became extremely scrupulous. Scrupulosity is a plague of "spiritual jitters" that only scrupulous Catholics understand. It took priestly counsel, much prayer and over two years to cure. By that time I was emotionally damaged and a spiritual cripple.

Becoming a Nun

Because of all these things, I seriously considered becoming a nun to save my soul and to serve God, Whom I thirsted after and longed to please in spite of discomfort in His company. I thought if I were a sister, God would give me a little more consideration at judgment. Nuns are called "spiritual brides" of Christ. That sounded pretty safe to me.

On December 8, 1966, I entered the Benedictine convent. At first I was thrilled with my new life. I desperately wanted to stay, but from the beginning, apprehension that I was not going to remain baffled me. Hovering over me like a taunting spirit, God drove me out of the convent shortly before Christmas. God used sleepless nights to deal with my will to remain.

One night I had a persistent thought that kept repeating, "Trust me, trust me." I came to understand by this message that great spiritual darkness lay ahead for me; Christ would be with me, but I would have to go on in faith. I was further led to believe that I had a missionary vocation. This was all so confusing and frightening that the next day I asked my novice mistress for permission to go to confession. After I related my experience to the priest, he told me that a long, dry spiritual darkness lay ahead and that I would have to go on faith alone.

Empty Ritual

A few days later I requested to leave and departed, broken and confused, planning to enter the Maryknoll Missionary Order in August. However, God had other plans. Upon discussing with the priest my departure from the convent, I was further bewildered when he told me I had no religious vocation at all! It was at this time that doubts about the validity of the Roman Church began to take hold of my thinking. When I told the same priest that I was losing my Catholic faith, he said, "You don't have to if you don't want to!" What next?

As time went on, I became increasingly unhappy. Mass, prayer, and the whole rigamarole were so empty and meaningless that I quit attending services, convinced at the same time that I would not go to hell if I missed Mass on purpose. I concluded that Catholicism was not what I thought it was, the pope was not infallible, and the Catholic Church did not have the complete truth, regardless of her claims. I knew I had a spiritual problem, but I also knew that no priest could help me.

As a result of all this, I personally excommunicated myself from Romanism and placed my spiritual dilemma confidently in God the Father's hands, trusting that He would show me the way.

A "Spiritual Prodigal"

For almost two years I was a "spiritual prodigal." During this time I married a Catholic, who shared my confusion. When our first child was born, I was troubled about baptism. Although I was a "fallen away" Catholic and had left the Church, remnants of her influence remained in my mind. So, wearily, I went to confession, attended Mass and received the sacraments. Then I had my son baptized. Feebly, I tried to repair my "Religious patchwork quilt". In spite of obedience to Church procedure after such a relapse, I still had no peace of soul and nothing helped. I prayed frantically for understanding and to be filled with the Holy Spirit. In a short time, God answered my prayers.

One day four years later, while praying for spiritual truth, I was directed to read the Bible. Shortly thereafter a Christian friend invited me to a Bible class. It was at this class that the Holy Spirit began the twigs for the nest He was building in my heart, waiting for His indwelling.

After ponderous Bible study and guidance from the preacher who taught the class, I began to see grievous contradictions between God's Word and the Roman Catholic Church. When reading Matthew 16:15-18, the Holy Spirit revealed to me that **Christ**, not Peter, was the "rock" on which the church was built! Since Christ was the **true** foundation, was Peter ever pope at all? In Mark 7: 9

71

Jesus said, "*Full well ye reject the commandment of God, that ye may keep your own tradition.*" I already knew that "popehood" was a Catholic tradition, so when the truth of this Scripture cut my heart, the pope literally toppled from his throne. Yet, I had no answer for my own personal salvation to take the place of the Catholic Church.

New Birth in Christ

One day at home while pondering John 5:24, "*Verily, verily I say unto you, He who heareth My words and believeth on Him who sent Me, hath everlasting life and shall not come into condemnation, but is passed from death unto life,*" the final link with Catholicism cracked

"*A born-again believer*"

and the chains of Rome fell. The Holy Spirit removed me from the jungle of Catholicism and placed me in the rich meadow of the Living Word, Jesus Christ. This is not man's doing but the gift of God by grace through faith. "*For by grace are ye saved through faith, and that not of yourself; it is the gift of God; not of works, lest any man should boast*" (Ephesians 2:8).

In place of my desire to be the spiritual bride of Christ as a nun, I was given the gift of a **new birth** and covered, not with the clothing of man, but with the righteousness of Christ, making me a child of God. "*But as many as received Him* [Jesus Christ], *to them gave He power to become the children of God, even to them that believe on His name; who were born, not of blood, nor of the will of the flesh, nor of the will of man, but of God*" (John 1:12-13). Jesus said, "*...Except a man be born again, he cannot see the kingdom of God*" (John 3:3).

As a born-again believer, I brought no robe of self-righteousness when I received Jesus into my life as **Savior**. Rather, He clothed me in His righteousness and presented me to the Father as one of the redeemed and heir of heaven **at that moment**.

Salvation in Christ Alone

I was at great peace spiritually after I found salvation in Christ by faith alone. Once I turned to Him by His grace, I never went to another Mass, never said a Rosary nor confessed to a priest. I knew that I was secure in Christ as it says in the Scriptures, *"These things have I written unto you that believe on the name of the Son of God, that ye may know that ye have eternal life, and that ye may believe on the name of the Son of God"* (1 John 5:13).

Other Scriptures that confirmed for me the truth that salvation is in Jesus Christ alone included Acts 4:12, *"Neither is there salvation in any other; for there is no other name under heaven given among men, whereby we must be saved."* And 1 Timothy 2:5, *"For there is one God, and one mediator between God and men, the man, Jesus Christ."* Mary also needed a Savior. In the Magnificat, she prayed, *"my spirit hath rejoiced in God my Savior"* (Luke 1:47).

God also showed me in Hebrews 10:10-14 that the Mass clearly was not ordained by Him for, *"...we are sanctified through the offering of the body of Jesus Christ once for all. And every priest standeth daily ministering and offering oftentimes the same sacrifices, which can never take away sins: But this man, after he had offered one sacrifice for sins forever, sat down on the right hand of God;...For by one offering he hath perfected forever them that are sanctified."*

There are no works that can save me or any person for it is *"not by works of righteousness which we have done, but according to his mercy he saved us, by the washing of regeneration, and renewing of the Holy Spirit"* (Titus 3:5). *"For God so loved the world, that he gave his only begotten Son, that whosoever believeth in him should not perish, but have everlasting life"* (John 3:16).

Proclaiming Truth

After I was born-again, I wrote to every Catholic priest and friend I knew, as well as to my novice mistress and told them the Gospel of Jesus Christ. With every Catholic whom I have come into contact since that time, I have tried to share the good news. For a year and a half I worked in a convent nursing home and continue to keep those dear sisters in my heart and prayers. For several years I have worked in a hospital, nursing homes and in private care as a nurse aide. Although I started training to become a licensed practical nurse, it did not work out for me. At present I am employed at the Caring Presence Home Health Care Agency giving all types of care and service to elderly people in their homes. I hope to have many opportunities to speak of Christ and His gift of salvation.

Another way I hope to bring glory to the Lord is by writing Christian children's stories and articles. At present, five have been selected for publication.

One of my first attempts to spread the Gospel was to write my testimony and print it in tract form. I did not know what I was going to do with those first thousand copies, but the Lord found a place for them all. Since then, I have had my story printed in Spanish and three languages of India, Hini, Telegu and Tamil-Nadu. It has been used extensively in the United States, India,  Ghana, Africa, Uganda and other English speaking countries. From the reports I have heard, our dear Lord has used my story of His grace, love and mercy to help many others. It has been printed in four magazines and two newsletters. This is totally the work of the Holy Spirit.

At present I am a member of Otis Baptist Church in Carlsbad, New Mexico, where my husband and I have lived since April 17, 1996. I have had training in Child Evangelism courses and

"I read and study my Bible"

taught Good News Clubs, Vacation Bible School and other groups. I read and study my Bible in depth, participate in many Bible studies and have read and continue to read many Christian books and magazines.

I have one son, James, and a dear daughter-in-law, Dana, who lives in Boise, Idaho. Both my son and his wife are born again and have been blessed with two children, a girl, Kaela, age six and Michael, age four. As a grandmother, it gives me much pleasure to share Christian books, videos, and other materials to help them grow in the knowledge of Jesus.

Peace and joy have increased as I have drawn closer to Christ and His Word. I thank Him with all my heart, soul and spirit for His gift of eternal life. Cooperating with His grace, I desire to speak for Him as He leads me. I pray that every Catholic will respond to the truth of God's Word that they may know Jesus Christ and the Truth will set them free.

Amy Bentley

The Conversion of a Catholic Nun: My Return to Christ

Knowing about Christ has been a round-about sort of thing for me because I became a Roman Catholic after being taught the truth as a child. It was the example and influence of my dear mother that eventually brought me to the relationship I have with God today. She saw to it that our family attended church regularly and we were taught the Word of God. How thankful I am for each and every day I spent at home with her when bronchial asthma had prevented me from attending school. I was still quite young when Mother was diagnosed with Huntington disease. Though placed in a nursing home, her encouragement and guidance was still consistent to the end. In spite of the difficulties, those times continue to be warmly cherished as the years pass.

Joining Catholicism and the Convent

When relatives from out of state offered to care for me, I left California for the Midwest. It was during my sophomore year of high school, at the age of sixteen, that I converted to Roman Catholicism. Convent life held promises of carrying the Gospel of Jesus Christ to others, a spiritual life, an excellent education, sisterly love and a home forever. So, after graduation, I became a Franciscan Sister where I served the Roman Catholic Church for twenty-four years. I applied myself to intense periods of training in meditation, prayer, the Gospel, vows of religion and physical overwork. In addition to college subjects I studied the sacraments of the Church, the commandments of God and the Church, the necessity of penance, and other aspects of spiritual life. The Bible was used to show the value of a virtuous life, but it was not fully taught nor was it considered to be the highest authority. The daily requirements of spiritual reading were centered around our espousal to the Church and Christ, rules and customs of the community, lives of the saints and vows. Because of my upbringing, I frequently used the Bible.

Observations

Not long after I began teaching school, my emphasis narrowed down to "The Church says versus the Bible says...." Often when students and parents questioned interpretations of Scripture, proof for the sacraments, origin of their prayers, Mass, rosary, etc., rather than having steadfast confidence in the teaching of Roman Catholicism, I found myself thinking that their questions were quite valid. I believed and tried to practice II Corinthains 4:2 where it says we are not to adulterate God's Word and that we are to "...*renounce the hidden things of dishonestly, not walking in craftiness, nor handling the word of God deceitfully*." The catechism lessons contained references to see the Bible, but there were seldom Bibles available. Whenever possible I used available finances for student Bibles and also encouraged students to request Bibles as gifts.

While practicing "obedience" in the convent, I sustained two back injuries. The result was severe pain whether sitting, standing, or lying down. There was very little relief even from traction or the back brace which I used for seven years. Yes, the proper care of a physician would have made a great difference, but requesting medical services was considered non-virtuous, a form of seeking attention. Of course we were made aware that doctor bills are usually very expensive. Those who did request medical care were likely to be penanced and admonished before others. (This was difficult for me to understand because the Church taught that it is a sin to neglect the care of the body.)

In time I became aware of how little inner peace there was in the lives of the sisters, how we lacked positive Christian love. It was common to be discouraged, to think negatively. Much time was spent job performing and attempting to control thoughts. Other convents were no different. While away from my own community for hospital lab studies, I had the opportunity to observe sisters from other religious orders. Stress, negative practices, and vows were all "on the rule book". Those who made any effort to correct the wrongs risked being penanced and life made even more difficult for them.

Vows

In time I did some research on the formation of religious foundations and vows within the Church. It was a surprise to learn that several religious professors actually taught that vows could not be binding in God's sight, for they were man-made. Rome has always allowed for revocations, but few know much about such things. Permission to leave the order would involve a formal letter of request to the "Reverend Mother" and "Holy Father" in Rome stating three reasons, but frequently the answer was no or was conditional.

From time to time we were warned about the danger of living in mortal sin should we ever leave. Yet, several sisters did receive dispensations. Others wanting to leave, could not. They either had no place to go or lacked the means to provide for themselves. Others were too ill to make such a drastic change.

Contradictions

It seemed that those in administration gloried in tyrannical authority, non-scriptural works and contradictions. They added to and changed the Word of God by impressing upon us the importance of vows as defined by men. While they bound us to "sanctify" ourselves through good works, they failed to teach verses like Ephesians 2:8-9, *"For by grace are ye saved through faith: and that not of yourselves: it is the gift of God; not of works, lest any man should boast."*

Our Church leaders taught a daily sacrifice, yet according to Hebrews 10:10 we are sanctified through the offering of Jesus *"once for all"*. It never occurred to me to question how the "true Church" could be filled with leaders who teach that the sacrifice of Calvary was incomplete.

It was many years before I realized that history clearly shows how the Roman Catholic Church denied the use of the Bible while teaching that "the Church" is infallible. It was not until after the Second Vatican Council that many Catholics, including priests and sisters, began studying the Scriptures.

I adhered strongly to my religious commitments while many sisters, brothers and priests left. But my eyes were eventually opened. I saw my Church:

- approving of and directing its members into such organizations as the World Council of Churches and the Masons,
- encouraging the Irish Mafia in their support of war in Northern Ireland and the Italian Mafia in supporting crime syndicates,
- backing the United Nations (which misrepresents peace in the United States and abroad),
- influencing Congress to legislate for One World Government (for inter-dependence, directly opposed to our American Constitution),
- papal donations to political and social organizations and causes while many religious communities are not even caring for their ill and elderly.

Courage to Leave

While my health continued to fail, I could see that my Church was failing its members spiritually. My partial paralysis was advancing. It was indeed a very difficult task to hobble about on crutches. In serious consideration of my situation I pondered deeply the advice of one priest: "If you have a bad investment, does one continue with it?" I watched how others adjusted after leaving. Many of them also left the Church. I wondered if breaking my vows would also mean spiritual death for me?

Finally on August of 1973, I did leave, but I remained within the Church, studying Scripture and comparing various churches and cults. I was concerned for Rome and hoped that somehow I could have a small part in a change from within. The more I studied, however, the more clearly I could see the radical difference between my Church and the fundamental truths of the written Word of God.

The Holy Spirit began to work in my thinking as I listened to Christian programs, read tracts, and met a few of my brother's Baptist friends. As it turned out, I had three appointments a week with my chiropractor, a non-practicing Catholic who was searching for the truth. When I made known to him my past position as a "religious" teacher and counselor in the parochial schools, the sessions turned to reading and comparing Bibles along with the treatments. I learned that this sincere man had studied with the Jehovah's Witnesses for two years and was intent upon going over to them. He was concerned with giving his two teenage daughters a better example and exposure to God's Word, something the Catholic school was not providing.

Back to Biblical Truth

As it turned out, he never did join them. He accepted an invitation to my brother's church for a special program and then returned the following Sunday for a regular service, which he continually praised with an air of satisfaction. Then another of his patients invited him to a church where Bart Brewer, an ex-priest from Mission To Catholics, was the special speaker. He brought me some of the Mission To Catholics literature and then I sent for more. Within a few days this ex-priest and another gentleman visited me, bringing the Word of God. Soon, they contacted me again to counsel me on trusting the Lord Jesus Christ and His written Word rather than remaining in a church which failed to teach the Bible.

The pain I had in sitting for any period held me back from committing myself to attend services. Also, as a member of two conservative groups fighting communism, I was hesitant to attend just any church for fear of getting into a liberal one. But that week the Holy Spirit worked and I accepted a ride to Mission Valley Community Chapel where Pastor Jim Mader faithfully teaches the Scriptures. His preaching emphasizes the need to be a born-again Christian, the virgin birth, the deity of Christ, being both God and man, coming to earth being born of a virgin, lived a sinless life, was crucified and died on a cross completing the sacrifice for sinful man, rose from the dead, and that He will soon return to take those who have received Him to glory and to judge those who reject Him. Since *"all have sinned, and come short of the glory of God"* (Romans 3:23), God has provided a gift which *"is eternal life through Jesus Christ our Lord"* (Romans 6:23).

Salvation at Last

As Sam (ex-Catholic) and Mary Mancino prayed for me and witnessed to me concerning these truths, I recalled hearing of them from my mother and at the Baptist church many years before. The following Sunday I raised my hand indicating my desire to receive the Lord Jesus Christ as my personal Saviour. Pastor Mader then visited and prayed with me at my apartment during the week. Expressing my desire to renounce Catholicism, I asked God's forgiveness for all my sin and I received Jesus Christ as my personal Lord and Saviour. That day in September of 1976, I found a peace that the Catholic Church had never given nor could ever give.

Now I have a contentment that can only be found in Jesus Christ and Him alone. He has satisfied my soul, something that twenty-four years in the convent, vows, sacrifices, Masses, rosaries, "offering it up", processions, saints, trifle traditions (from pagan-adopted practices), mixed-up theological debates, and a controlled religious system could never begin to do. It is the written Word of God that showed me the way, not Roman Catholicism.

Some may think that those years were a waste of time or that I might feel bitterness for all the hardship in a false religious system. I can honestly say I do not feel even a slight bitterness nor do I consider one moment a waste of time. I know that God had a purpose in allowing it all. I do, however, feel sorrow for Roman Catholics (especially the "religious") because they do not consistently study and they incorrectly interpret the Bible and do not know biblical salvation.

Overwhelmed by Jesus' love for me, my thanksgiving and praise is ever before Him. I manage even though my health is still not good. I know that Jesus will always keep me close to Him, for that is the desire of my heart. I also desire and pray for you who read my story that you may be touched by His Spirit, that you will hunger and thirst for His righteousness and that you will be filled as you study, believe, and obey the Bible.

Rocio P. Zwirner

The Woman at the Well

The youngest in a family of four brothers and four sisters, I am a Spaniard who was born in Madrid. My family was profoundly involved in the Roman Catholic Church. One of my aunts, Maria Josefa Segovia, was the co-founder of a secular religious order, the *Institucion Teresiana,* dedicated to education.

"Of all my brothers and sisters, I'm the last"

My Early Years

At the age of two, I was taken along with two of my sisters to a convent boarding school. During the week, we lived in a house with members of the order who worked as public school teachers. On weekends we went home. Sometimes my mother visited us at the school in the afternoon and helped to feed us dinner. From age two to age seven, I was there acquiring my basic education. In the house there was a small chapel with an altar and tabernacle. There, from the time I was very small, I began to be conscious of all the religious practices of Roman Catholicism. I was taught to pray, to use holy water, and to follow the ritual of the Mass and the rest of the sacraments.

I made my first confession before a priest at the age of five and prepared for my first communion at age six. At this same age I began to read and write and to memorize the Catholic catechism of Astete in order to enjoy the privilege of Holy Communion. I remember clearly how expectantly I prepared for this event, firmly convinced that Jesus was really in the consecrated host and would

enter into my heart. I thank the Lord that He gave me a delicate conscience and a sensitivity to everything related to Him.

From my infancy, Jesus was the motive of my dreams, aspirations, and desires. He was my intimate Friend. I was taught about God, the Trinity, and Jesus Christ by both the Teresians and my family. I knew about the lives of many saints and martyrs, the history of the early church (according to the Catholic Church), exemplary lives of all time periods and many stories of Bible characters.

"The day of my First Communion"

All of this motivated me with a desire to imitate their lives. I sincerely wanted to please God and dedicate my life to Him. I fervently worked to comply with all the ordinances of the church: daily Mass, confession, communion, fasting, alms, prayers for the dead in purgatory, indulgences, etc. We recited the rosary both at home and at school. I had private times of prayer and endeavored to be a regular helper in the sacristy of the school chapel.

When I was seven, I went to several different private schools for girls, in Madrid, in the mountain chain of Cordoba in the south of Spain, in Avila, in the province of Castilla, the city of "Saints and Knights", and in Burgos. Always living far from family, each time I moved I was more attached to my special friendship with the Lord.

A Private Vow

At the age of fourteen, I felt the call to consecrate myself to the Lord, wanting to be totally His. I asked permission of my confessor to make a private vow of chastity. One of the happiest days of my life was January 21, 1961, when I committed myself to the Lord by this vow. I also put on a special "engagement" ring. After this, my purpose became definite; I decided to be a missionary. I proceeded to finish my secondary education with a goal to study nursing to be more useful on the mission field.

When I finished school at seventeen and told my family of my desire to be a missionary and to study nursing, I received no encouragement. They told me they could not help me financially and expected me to find employment, the sooner the better.

Unfettered Liberty

I had a difficult adolescence after I finished school. Although I was living with my family, I began to enjoy liberties I never had had. I began to have problems which I did not have the strength or spiritual maturity to face. Although I tried to find refuge and strength in the sacraments, as I had been taught, I was powerless, vulnerable, and lost in the "new" life the world offered me. I felt overwhelmed by my repeated sins and complete lack of control. I began to work and make money, but my family's financial needs did not permit me to save enough for nursing school.

I smoked, drank, and never passed up a chance to enjoy life in one manner or another. Sometimes I was in total anguish because I felt so separated from the Lord. My confessor, an Augustinian priest, had scruples about giving me absolution for my sins because I was always repeating the same things over and over again. My situation was so desperate that more than once I was at the point of wanting to commit suicide.

A New Confessor

One day I came from church and in my distress entered running and crying into the Dominican monastery. A priest passed by the corner where I had hid myself and asked why I was crying. I started to talk with him. He waited patiently for my answers. He counseled me and offered the absolution for which I was so anxious, but that had been refused to me for, according to the Catholic religion, without the blessing of the priest, God would not pardon me. After that day the Dominican priest, P. Juan Luis Tena, was my confessor and helped me.

Entering the Convent

When I was almost eighteen, the minimum age to enter the novitiate for the Combonianos Missionaries, I had a sudden change of mind and decided to become a cloistered nun. I was referred to the Convent of the Clarissas, the "Monastery of the Sacred Heart", in Cantalapiedra, Salamanca, because my confessor's mother and five of his sisters were at that same place. Soon I began to correspond with the nuns, especially with Sister Mary Grace. We decided that within a few months, I would go to the convent.

When I broke the news to my parents, they did not want to give their permission. This created a big problem in my family, but finally after much struggle, they gave their permission. I left for the convent on February 4, 1965.

I cannot describe the inner joy and expectations with which I entered this new life. On the other hand, there was sadness because of the opposition of my parents, especially that of my mother when she tried to release me to that which I had always desired, to be the Lord's totally and completely.

Religious Life

I adapted to the religious life of "poverty, chastity, obedience and Cloister (solitude)". The first and most inconvenient problem that I encountered was the cold. In these convents, the austerity and poverty of life was translated into complete denial of any material and personal convenience. One has to submit to the Lord by means of rules, work, prayer, discipline, sacrifices, and even bodily self-imposed suffering. There was no contact with the world, nothing that would gratify or satisfy the senses. Whether cold or hot, hungry or thirsty, discomfort, humiliation, want, etc., one pretends that she is in a room filled with roses. I don't know about my convent sisters, but it seemed to me as nothing compared to pleasing the Lord and making my salvation and the salvation of other souls sure. We had to be "co-redeemers with Jesus and Mary". To intercede for the living and the dead, we were the dynamo, the hidden heart of the Holy Catholic Church. Our life of prayer and voluntary suffering was the key to success in the Christian life.

At last I was sure (or so I thought) that I had "arrived" in a secure harbor where I could practice all the sacraments. I was living a holy life separated from the evil and mundane. I prayed, worked, made special acts of self-imposed suffering, constant sacrifices and kept the rules of the convent, the religious life, and the Church. What more could the Lord ask that we had not already given? Apparently I was obedient, a hard worker, honest, completely dedicated to the glory of God.

In August of 1965, I took the habit of the Clarissas. One year later I made my first temporary vows and three years later the solemn and final vows. Now officially and permanently, I was consecrated to the Lord—"married" to the Lord or so I was taught.

"The day I took the habit of Clarissa"

My Godmother's Gift

The day I was to take the habit, my family was invited to the ceremony. I was admitted to the Franciscan Order of the Clarissas on August 8, 1965. My family name was changed to "Sister Maria of the Holy Spirit". Along with my parents, sisters and brothers, my baptismal godmother, Ma. Antonia Ruiz, was invited also. She gave me a Bible and with the Mother Superior's permission, I began to read it. At first I read it from cover to cover but sometimes there were many things I did not understand. I enjoyed reading the New Testament more than the Old Testament. Because I wanted so much to know the Lord and love Him, I constantly read this precious book and also consulted sections of the Divine Office which were written in Latin. I took note of the references to the book of Psalms that we recited daily and in my free time read in Spanish. Because I had studied Latin in secondary school, soon it was possible for me to understand and translate it.

Thirsting for the Lord

The Gospel of John was read most assiduously by me during the nine years that I spent in the convent. I didn't understand the significance of salvation, but did come to know more about Who was speaking to me: "*I am the Good Shepherd*", or "*I am the Door*", "*I am the Way, the Truth, the Life*", "*He that is thirsty, come to Me and drink*". I particularly delighted in and meditated on the encounter Jesus had with the Samaritan woman at the well (John 4:1-26).

In the center of the convent there was a well which was surrounded by flowers and bushes. Many times I would sit there and pray, ardently desiring the presence of Jesus with all my mind, being, and will. "Lord, give me to drink, I thirst for Thee. Please give me living water!"

With the passing of the years, I was more and more dissatisfied with myself. I wanted to be better day after day, but how? How could I satisfy my Lord? How could I grow more and more in holiness? It was a struggle and an anxiety to the point that I was becoming unbalanced physically and emotionally.

I saw in the Gospel of John, in the prayer of the Last Supper when Jesus prayed for His own that He said, "*I pray not that thou shouldest take them out of the world, but that thou shouldest keep them from the evil*" (John 17:15). In my desire for holiness, I saw in the same prayer, "*Sanctify them through thy truth; thy word is truth*" (John 17:17).

"The Convent separated from the world"

In the convent we were totally separated from the world, virtually on another planet. Yet in the same passage I read, "*As thou hast sent me into the world, even so have I also sent them into the world*" (John 17:18). We wanted to make ourselves believe that cloistered nuns were the "cream of the cream" of religious life. With the passing of time, however, I met with more and more contradictions to this view. There were too many rules and practices that were the same as those of the Pharisees who so despised the Lord. Distinctions were made between nuns and visitors, between

"As a bride of Christ with my family inside the convent"

rich and poor families. Many times I heard the statement that a "white" lie used to save a difficult situation or to defend something or someone is to make good use of "the left hand" and therefore is not a sin. Rules and traditions and rigidity of obedience incapacitated one to make decisions. Things were always well-protected for appearances and there was a formality of innumerable regulations.

Struggle Within

A great struggle began between what my mind was learning about God, the spiritual life, and the life we were living in the convent. This struggle brought me to the point of physical illness. I was taken to the doctor because I suddenly lost my voice. The Mother Superior thought that I had tuberculosis of the throat, as was the case with another nun at that time.

Yet another nun, because of her distress of mind threw herself into the convent's well. Her cries, not for help but of inconsolable mental torment, were heard throughout the entire convent, "I'm condemned, I'm condemned". She didn't know how to swim, yet she was floating and we were able to take her out alive. Her panic because of eternal condemnation gave me food for thought. During "Operation Rescue", Mother Superior kept repeating, "My daughter, stop condemning yourself" but the nun kept on wailing, "I'm condemned". Even now I remember this terrible experience with pain, for many still follow the same path, believing in what is dead and empty.

Of my nine years in the convent, the last three were spent in an internal struggle that had no respite. I could not understand how at first I had been so happy and now I had absolutely no contentment.

I asked help of the spiritual father of my aunt, the Teresiana nun. Father Amalio Valcarcel was at that time the secretary to the Master General of the Dominican Fathers in Rome. In His providence, God permitted the priest to make a trip to Spain and he took advantage of that opportunity to visit me in the convent. After hearing what was happening to me and that I preferred to die rather than to renounce my monastic life, he told me something very simple that helped me understand and make a final decision.

With much compassion and patience he said, "My daughter, does it not seem to you that you have known God at least a little bit in these years of religious life?" "Yes," I answered. "Then, don't you believe that God is more of a Father and Mother to you than your own parents, that He doesn't want to torture you, and that if He wants you to be here, He will give you the necessary happiness and peace to persevere in this way of life?"

On Eagle's Wings

I admitted with a broken heart that I could not continue in peace. Father Valcarcel took it upon himself to convince the Mother Superior to let me go for a while to the home of my parents to determine what God's will was for my life. They asked permission of the Bishop of Salamanca. I was permitted to leave and to stay with my family for a set length of time after which I had to decide whether to return to the convent or to solicit secularization through the Pontifical Curia in Rome.

When my family learned of this decision, they hurried to come and get me. That day in March of 1974 I thought I would die. Never in all my life, before or after, have I suffered such profound sorrow. I was in indescribable agony. They did not let me say good-bye to the nuns who had been my dear "sisters" during these years. With a cold and sorrowful benediction, the Mother Superior, with two sisters of the board, accompanied me to the door of the convent. The sound of each turn of the locks and doors were like blows to my heart. I couldn't believe what was happening, that my dear Lord was letting me go. I believed I was abandoning Him. Wasn't He all-powerful? Could He not stop the process? Did He not know how I loved Him and that this separation made me fearful? Where was He in this hour? As a devouring fire within me, my heart cried, "My God, my God, why have You abandoned me?"

In order to leave, my sisters had to support me by the arms because my feet would not support me. I was unable to speak, only able to cry. Without strength, I was taken to Madrid under a black sky that also cried in a torrential rain erasing the silhouette of the convent hidden on the horizon. Where was my God?

Blind in my life of vanity and sin, I did not see the powerful and loving arms of God taking me out of these circumstances to offer me the salvation for which I longed, if only I could find it! As it is written in Deuteronomy 32:10-12, *"He found him in a desert land, and in the waste, howling wilderness; he led him about, he instructed him, he kept him as the apple of his eye. As an eagle stirreth up her nest, fluttereth over her young, spreadeth abroad her wings, taketh them, beareth them on her wings, So the Lord alone did lead him, and there was no strange god with him."*

Life on the Outside

My adjustment to new life on the outside world was slow and difficult. I was disconnected from everything and everyone. Noises of everyday life were, among other things, a source of stress to me. I was twenty-seven years old and as immature as an adolescent that faced life for the first time. Without the protection of the habit and the "intonation" of the rules and regulations that resounded like the convent bells, I was easy prey to my own sinful nature that for so many years had been insulated from reality under the cloak of religious "good works".

I had no power in me, no discernment, no direction. Foolishly believing that the Lord had abandoned me, I rebelled against any form of rules and regulations. I was not even able to attend Church. It seemed empty to me, making me feel restless inside, estranging me more and more from all religious practice. I was not able to go to Mass, communion, confession, or even read the Bible. These things not only had no meaning to me, they perturbed me. Soon I began to smoke and drink and to dress myself without modesty. I struggled against my conscience, wanting to do most of the time what I knew was against the law of God and everything moral.

Still desiring to study to be a nurse, this time my family helped me. The school of nursing I was to attend was far from Madrid and far from my family, in the city of Barcelona in the northeast of Spain. Again, I moved away and began to study. Although the pursuit of this career gave me much satisfaction, I knew that in my personal life I was losing control of myself and slipping into deep depression.

The High Cost of Ungodly Counsel

It was recommended to me that I counsel with a psychiatrist who was also a priest. Unfortunately the cure was worse than the sickness. The counsel given under professional and priestly authority put me in the most dangerous situation of my life. When I told him my personal history and what I had left, he counseled that it was "necessary therapy" to be "myself". "All your life you have been very repressed; you must give yourself the opportunity to be open; let your instincts and desires give you enjoyment of life that you have never had. Lie, rob if you want, get angry if necessary, fornicate, drink, smoke (he smoked enthusiastically as he gave me counsel), enjoy yourself with men, don't bury yourself with study on the weekends, go out, have a good time, etc. Don't worry, don't think about what is sin and what isn't. If your conscience troubles you, throw your guilt on me, roll it on my shoulders." "But Father," I said, "this is against the law of God." "Don't worry," he answered, "this is for your well-being, it's part of your therapy."

I spent those years studying nursing and "recuperating" personally at a very high cost. At the same time that I was building a career, my spiritual and personal life was deteriorating more and more. My conscience was being seared.

I passed the summer in Puerto Rico in the home of my brother and another summer in England, never missing an opportunity to have a good time and "see the world". It was a season full of abandonment and personal self-destruction.

A Papal Visit

On finishing my nursing studies and obtaining a degree, my parents gave me a trip to Italy as a graduation gift with a view to my visiting the Pope. I arrived in Rome in August of 1978. The Dominican father that helped me leave the convent was waiting, for my parents had alerted him. He accompanied me on my tour through the "holy city", and gave me a special ticket to attend one of the Pope's audiences. I did not really want to go but, since I did not want to offend the priest by turning down the invitation, I went. The entire performance seemed a ridiculous show. I abhorred all the veneration and enthusiasm for a mere man. Looking at the crowd, I could not understand what was going on with them. I wanted to run away as far as I could; I was ashamed of this hysterical gathering. Even though I had taken no active part in the activities, I considered the luxury, pomp, artifice and empty words an insult to God and repugnant to me. I wanted to go home as soon as possible to my own country. In Assisi, I made a general confession, trying to reconcile myself with the Lord. I attended Mass. This new fervor lasted only until my return to Spain, at which time I promptly returned to my old way of life.

From Puerto Rico to the Dominican Republic

In this situation, with so many problems, and looking in vain for permanent employment as a nurse, I decided to go to another country to pursue my nursing career. I went to Puerto Rico where my brother had lived for some years. He offered me his hospitality and help while I got on my feet. Once again, with a broken heart, I left family, friends, and country.

I spent some difficult months in this beautiful isle of the Caribbean, trying to find work and to establish permanent American residency. Because of bureaucratic procedures, both objectives took more time than indicated by immigration authorities. It became imperative that I leave U.S. soil, at least for the time being. Desperate, I thought of returning to almost any part of Europe and joining some counter-culture group to lose myself somewhere or perhaps to perish. Why keep up the struggle? I was at the end of my rope.

My brother, knowing something of the possibilities I was considering, suggested that I go to find work in the Dominican Republic. He was sure that I would find employment there because of the scarcity of graduate nurses in that country. Meanwhile, he would continue working to obtain a resident American visa for me so I could return to Puerto Rico.

Without much enthusiasm, I assented to his proposal and left straightaway for the Dominican Republic in September of 1981. In Santo Domingo I quickly made new friends and got a fairly good position in one of the best clinics in the city. I began to feel a little more cheerful and hopeful. It was at the clinic that I encountered Christian believers for the first time. They were a couple who invited me to a Bible study and then to a service at their church. Attending a Protestant service was a new and exciting experience I did not want to pass up.

A Conviction of Sin

The Saturday evening before the appointed Sunday I was to attend church with this couple, I went out for supper and dancing with one of my friends, a divorced doctor who had an entertaining evening in mind. My conscience was entreating me not to go out with this man, but rebellious and weak as usual, I went out to enjoy myself as much as possible. Early in the morning, however, while crossing the street, I heard the strident crow of a rooster. Suddenly, it was like a sword had pierced my soul. I immediately remembered Peter denying Jesus. I could stand no more. Leaving the "friend" standing there, I ran down the street crying, not knowing where I was, only looking up to heaven and screaming for help and pardon. From the depths of my being I cried to God, "Save me, help me, I can't do it alone. I am lost without You, please pardon me and save me!" Without my knowing it, the Holy Spirit had commenced His work in me by means of the conviction of sin.

I had to ask directions to find my way to my apartment. I was, in every sense of the word, **lost** in the middle of the night in a big city. But now, the Great Consoler was with me. The following day, I collected myself to go to the Sunday service to which the couple had invited me. It was a recently organized fundamentalist Baptist church whose pastor was an American missionary, Paul Joles. The service was held in the living room of his house. When I arrived in the middle of the Sunday School class, they were talking about the Holy Spirit. That morning was the continuation of what had happened the night before when my conversion had really begun. Now I began to "see" and to "understand" what had been before "veiled" to me. Christ, through His Word, caused me to understand the plan of salvation, "...*that Christ died for our sins according to the scriptures; and that he was buried, and that he rose again the third day according to the scriptures*" (1 Corinthians 15:3-4). Having been convicted of sin by God's Word, confirming that we are all sinners (Romans 3:23, Isaiah 59:2), that sin is separation from God (Romans 3:26), and that this separation leads to death and certain judgment (Hebrews 9:27, II Thessalonians 1:8-9), the Lord did not leave me there.

There is a solution: Jesus Christ. He paid the penalty for our sins and is the way to God (I Timothy 2:5-6, I Peter 3:18). Salvation is the precious gift of His grace (Ephesians 2:8-9, John 3:16). How wonderful is the grace of God which is so mercifully offered to all who believe in Him! Amazing grace, that He lifted me from darkness into His marvelous light, from sin to pardon, from death to life! Grace that found a lost sheep and brought the prodigal daughter home to the embrace of the Father Who receives me with unconditional love.

How can I express what happened that morning! Exploding from grief turned into joy, a flood of tears flowed from my broken spirit and I fell at the feet of Jesus. Like the woman at the well, I was cleansed and given living water. I knew this was the new birth that gave me life in Him and liberty that I had never known. The words spoken from the cross, "*It is finished*" (John 19: 30), were understood. Jesus is the Lamb of God that takes way the sin of the world (John 1:29). At the same time, He is our High Priest and Intercessor, the Propitiation (completely satisfactory payment) for sin.

"The veil fell from my eyes"

The veil fell from my eyes and I saw that I was accepted in Christ. So many things happened. This was the Christ I had longed to know, to love and to serve, the God of the Bible Who saves through His redeeming Blood shed once for all, Christ Jesus Who does not need the help of sacraments, personal works, nor priests and saints to intercede or redeem me. He gives the gift of salvation by His sufficient and holy grace, if we believe in Him.

I started to take the first steps in my new life in Christ: the study of the Bible, and the baptism of the believer, my first public testimony. A long letter was written to the priest in Spain, the one who helped me leave the convent. I shared with him the joy of my faith and my new life guided by the Lord. These were clear evidences that I belonged to Christ and not to some religion.

Living Water

When the missionary-pastor who preached the Word when I had been born-again by grace was called to the United States, he gave me a word of advice and the best warning I had ever received: "Read your Bible every day, whether you feel like it or not, because through the Word of God you will find all that is necessary to continue persevering and growing in the Lord and for all that you may need." I faithfully followed this advice without much effort because I had an insatiable thirst to know more and more about the Holy Scriptures. In this way, I drew nearer and nearer to God and discovered His will for my life. Today, I can say that thanks to the

Lord's grace, I have read the Bible through sixteen times, once for each year since my conversion. What a tremendous blessing!

My desire for the Word of God motivated me enough to enter the Quisqueyan Bible Institute in Santo Domingo. The founder and director of that institute was another American Missionary, Rev. Larry Dobson. There I was able to follow a systematic study of the Word, enjoying the privilege of being a student in a healthy and joyful atmosphere under teaching according to biblical principles and doctrines.

The in-depth study of the Scriptures brought great peace and emotional stability in my life even though I had to work and study very hard. This effort was a joy, not a burden. Knowing and living by the Word of God is an inexhaustible source of blessings. In my own life I was beginning to realize what Paul declared, *"...I live, yet not I, but Christ liveth in me"* (Galatians 2:20).

"With my parents when I finished nursing school"

In my past life as a Catholic nun, I wanted to do everything. I struggled to be better. I sacrificed myself to the extreme, to win, to help Christ save the lost souls, to do everything well enough to buy my way to heaven. What was happening now? Christ has done it for me, Christ saves me, Christ produces good works in my life so I can do them to please Him, not to buy His approval. *"For we are his workmanship, created in Christ Jesus unto good*

"Santo Domingo, taking care of abandoned children"

works, which God hath before ordained that we should walk in them" (Ephesians 2:10). What a joyous discovery! Thank you, Lord.

Serving the Lord

While studying the Scriptures during the second year at the institute in Santo Domingo, I felt the Lord's calling to dedicate myself completely to His service. With my diploma of a "Christian Worker" I sought the Lord's will as to the area where I could serve Him. I visited my parents in Spain, leaving myself open to the Lord's work in my country. When this attempt proved fruitless, I returned to Santo Domingo and decided to start with something I had desired for a long time yet was never able to accomplish. I decided to open the doors of my heart and my house to the abandoned or parentless children wherever I could find them, or whenever circumstance brought them to me. With the approval of the local church and the pastor, I began this ministry and soon had a board of directors composed of various couples from the church.

The children started to arrive at my home in a providential manner. Surprisingly, many of them only a few months old, others just a few years old. In three years, we had eleven small children ranging up to nine years of age. With the children came pressures and economic problems. Even bigger were the spiritual problems and battles which took place with the weariness of being alone. The attacks of the enemy grew oppressively worse. In the same measure, the providence and generosity of our Lord helped us to resolve our difficulties and to continue our work. In a real way, I was able to experience and rejoice in the words, *"I know Whom I have believed"* (II Timothy 1:12).

He is Faithful

There is another important chapter in this testimony that I want to share with you because it may help someone understand how the Lord operates for good in all the details of life. Sometimes, when a religious person such as a Catholic, leaves the "consecrated" life and returns to the "world", and gets married, in the religious atmosphere this is almost taken as an offense, as though the departure from religious life were purely for sexual motives. How sad!

I wanted to be totally consecrated to the Lord. Catholic teaching instructs about the **marvels** and **privileges** of celibacy, pretending that this manner of single life for the love of God exceeds in honor and virtue that of marriage. After my conversion to Christ, in the light of the Scriptures, I learned how erroneous and false the teaching and practice of celibacy is.

The Holy Bible from the beginning teaches how God, as He created all things, saw that **everything** He created was **good**, including man. But the first time God said that something was **not good** was when he saw that man was alone! *"And the Lord God said, It is not good that the man should be alone; I will make him an help fit for him"* (Genesis 2:18). In all the Old Testament, marriage is the **normal** condition of man and woman; in the New Testament, Paul, in the first letter to Timothy, speaks of the signs of apostasy, pointing out that one of them would be the **prohibition to marry** (I Timothy 4: 1-5). In naming the qualifications of a bishop, Paul assumes the candidate is married (1 Timothy 3:2).

Years before I went into the convent, I arrived at a point at which I wanted no man in my life. I broke off with my then boyfriend for fear of loving God less. I had been taught that one could live a "cleaner" and more dedicated life to serve the Lord when in the single state. All this, however high-sounding it may seem, is not supported by the Scriptures! No man or institution has

"*Our wedding day*"

the right to demand celibacy in order to be able to serve in the ministry of the church. Most of the godly men and women of the Bible were married. If anyone decides not to marry, it is to be of his own free will, not something imposed from the outside. Exceptions such as the prophet, Jeremiah, were single with a determined purpose from the Lord, not from human sources or institutions as was the case with ancient pagan practices of celibacy in the worship of idols. Later this

practice was established by the Catholic Church. In Matthew 19: 11-12, Jesus declares that the decision in life to be single is made freely under a special call.

From the time of my conversion, I had been praying to the Lord that He would provide me with a good Christian husband who would protect me and be my spiritual leader in my new Christian life. Year after year with many difficulties, I was praying and waiting for the Lord's reply. The life of a single woman is neither easy nor secure, especially far from family and the protection of a church or mission organization. I was now in my forties and had responsibility for the care of eleven children and the orphanage. Who in his right mind would marry anyone living in that scenario? It seemed to be a lost cause.

But God is faithful and gracious, and once more He demonstrated His paternal love in an incredible way in my life. From four thousand miles away, He provided the man that He had prepared for me. One fine day in January of 1990, I received a letter from an unknown American that had heard of me in a church in his home state of Oregon through missionaries who told of trips they had made to the Dominican Republic. This man, a widower, alone some five years, decided that same day to

"With my dear husband"

write me a letter. He stated in his letter that he very much wanted to meet me. It all began this way. We soon wrote letters back and forth and made some telephone calls. Three months later he visited me in Santo Domingo. I remember my first words to him when we met in the airport, "Welcome to my life!" We fell deeply in love with one another, a confirmation of what God had already arranged. Two weeks later we were engaged to be married. On June 22, 1990, two months later, we were married in Corvallis, Oregon. What a joy and blessing!

My husband is the external manifestation of God's love in my life. He is God's "umbrella" of protection and guidance, my spiritual leader, the expression of His tender and merciful love. Through this union, He made a tremendous change in my life, filling it with abundance, joy, security, and indescribable peace. For these reasons, I wanted to include this personal aspect of my life in this testimony.

Only in obedience to the Word of God in **all** His counsel do we find the Rock, the stability and the joy of Christian living. Not only in this life but in the life that follows, we will praise Him with His angels and the other saints through all eternity. He is faithful to His promises (John 3:16 and John 5: 24).

Let me conclude by appropriating the words of the apostle Paul found in Romans 1:16-17, *"For I am not ashamed of the gospel of Christ; for it is the power of God unto salvation to everyone that believeth; to the Jew first, and also to the Greek. For in it is the righteousness of God revealed from faith to faith; as it is written, the just shall live by faith."*

"I am not ashamed of the Gospel of Christ."

Alicia Simpson

Alicia: My Search for Peace, a Nun's Story

The testimony of Alicia Simpson is summarized from her book published in 1989. Her story is taken from a talk she gave before she died in which she desired to be faithful in recording what God had done for her. The setting is primarily in the convent and between World War I and World War II. It is an account of tragedy, frustration, and human failure which is given in a spirit of gratitude for the genuine life-changing impact of Jesus Christ which transformed her. Alicia proclaims the present reality of assurance: God's transforming power is available to all who are drawn to seek Him.

Childhood Memories

I was born into a Roman Catholic household. As a child I knew nothing but abuse and ill-treatment from a mother, a father and then a step-father, of whom I was terrified. Because they were people well-known in business and musical circles, their cruelty was never discovered.

When the time came for schooling, I was sent to a convent. It was run by nuns whose lives were dedicated to the Blessed Virgin Mary. The emphasis of the religious education was on devotion to Our Lady. Great stress was laid on the fact that, after confession of one's sins to a priest, salvation depended almost entirely upon the intercession of the Mother of God. We addressed her by countless titles.

At the age of eighteen, I made a desperate attempt at suicide. Since I was under-age and my mother did not want me back, I was placed in the charge of a Roman Catholic probation officer. Without home, friends, or money, I consented to go to the convent which the probation officer assured me would be ideal for recovery.

Convent Days

The probation officer took me to the convent. I would not see the outside world again until I was thirty-six. Inside this 'religious institution' such things as Christian love, mercy, kindness and concern for one another were unknown. It was a place of hard work, unspeakable living conditions, and severe punishment. We had to do penance in order to try to earn forgiveness for our sins. We had to work in strict silence, even our scanty meals were eaten in silence while someone read from the lives of the saints.

Only on Sundays were we allowed to read anything for ourselves, unless we had been deprived of the privilege as a punishment. Our reading matter was exclusively Roman Catholic books. In all the years I was shut away, I never saw a newspaper. No one knew what was going on on the outside.

When I realized how I had been tricked, I suddenly came to life again. Life became sweet, and I now wanted to hang on to it and to get out. If I did get out, where would I go? The nuns knew well that I was without a friend in the world and that no one would ever come and claim me. In the end, I resigned myself to being there for the rest of my life.

I turned to the only consolation that was left for me—religion. This consisted for the most part of praying to statues and pictures of the Blessed Virgin Mary and the saints. I believed that all this devotion was the right way to go about getting peace with God. As a Roman Catholic, I was striving after something that eluded me.

The Search for Peace

In the convent I was eventually made a Child of Mary as a reward for good conduct. However, in spite of accepting the hardships of my life as a penance for what I had done, try as I would, I could not get peace with God nor feel any forgiveness for my sins. No matter what I did, that barrier remained between me and that dread Being up there of whom I was so afraid.

The years went by and time became meaningless. I don't remember now what age I was when the idea first entered my head that I wanted to become a nun. Surely if I could become a nun and live a life of complete dedication to God, I could earn forgiveness for my sins and find the right way to peace with Him.

How was I to become a nun? I had no money and girls and women who wished to enter Roman Catholic religious orders usually had to take a sum of money in with them as a dowry, since they were becoming "brides of Christ", but I hadn't a penny. I had no position in life, no friends or relations to pull strings on my behalf, and I was in a most unrespectable situation for anyone wanting to be a nun.

In the end I was allowed to make my request known to Mother Superior. To my great joy at the time, she told me that there was just one religious order open to someone like me—a strictly enclosed Third Order of Carmelites, a very penitential order. I was transferred and eventually became known as Sister Magdalene of the Passion. I entered with full enthusiasm and great ideas, but I did not find the kind of life I had expected. Nor did I find what I had gone to seek—peace with God.

First Steps to Freedom

There seemed to be so much 'performance' of religion and so little of anything that was real. Deep down inside me was the desire for something deeper, a longing for something that was eluding me. I did not know what it was, but something was causing me the greatest uneasiness and dissatisfaction. An inner conviction was telling me I was in the wrong place.

Years ago it was considered a great scandal for an enclosed nun to return to the world after being clothed with the habit of an order and pronounced 'the bride of Christ'. There was one thing, however, I had not done: I had not taken final vows, and nothing would induce me to do so. I began to question obedience to religious superiors and many other things. Being in a Protestant country, and not having taken my final vows, I could not be kept against my will, but I had much to go through before I was released.

At thirty-six years of age, I came out of the convent into a world of war in the heart of London, which was getting the worst of it. This was the first step taken on my journey toward finding peace with God. I was in disgrace with Holy Mother Church and sickened with religion which had failed me.

Almost immediately, my age group had to register for war work and, not wishing to go into the armed services, I was sent to airplane engineering. I was bitter, disillusioned, friendless, homeless and penniless. I was under the continual strain of war. Though I could hardly have cared less at the time as buildings crashed around me, again and again my life was preserved and brought out of the shadow of death. To be killed in an air-raid, without the knowledge of salvation, was not in God's plan for me.

An Unhappy Marriage

Soon I was transferred to Scotland on war work and there I eventually met a man, a widower, who asked me to marry him. For the first time in my life I was being offered a chance of security, a home of my own, a name, an opportunity to settle down and take root somewhere. The offer was too good to refuse. This man was a Protestant, very 'religious', an elder of his church but, like myself knew nothing of salvation.

Things went from bad to worse, and I bitterly regretted the step I had taken in such haste. I began to think that the misery of my married life was a punishment from God for what I had done by marrying outside the Church of Rome. The more I thought about it, the more I longed once again to try to get right with God.

On the Run

While my husband had gone fishing for a weekend, I went to Manchester. I had never been there before but I knew it had a convent of the same order in which I had been. I told my story to the Mother Superior, expressed my great desire to get to confession and declared my intention to stay in the convent, this time for good.

The next three to four days were spent in a small room. The Mother Superior did not come back to see me and no word came from the Bishop who had to be consulted because I was married in the eyes of the law. One afternoon while I was sitting reading the life of a saint, I was convicted that I was to go back to my husband. I put my few belongings in my case, put on my hat and coat and made it out the front door.

Still convinced that I was to return to my husband, I sent him a telegram to meet me at Glasgow Central. If he did not come, I would not even have bus fare to where we lived. When the train drew into the central station there he was standing on the platform! He was so glad to see me, he did not ask where I had been. Again I had made an attempt to find peace with God, but had gone the wrong way about it. *"There is a way which seemeth right unto a man, but the end thereof are the ways of death"* (Proverbs 14:12).

A Temporary Respite

We talked things over and decided that we would try once more to make a go of our marriage. For my husband's sake, I attended his church. This was merely an outward gesture for I certainly was not going to unite in worship with heretics or handle the forbidden book, the Bible. At heart, I was still a convicted Roman Catholic and knew nothing of salvation or the new creation to be found through Jesus Christ.

Once again our marriage began to come undone. In desperation, I started to make plans to run away again. This time I would not go to a convent. I intended to seek all the things my marriage had not given me. Only a lack of money held me back.

Divine Intervention

Into this hopeless situation, God intervened. We were as lost as any two people can be: a religious man who did not know he was lost and an ex-religious woman who knew well that she was helpless. Does not our Lord Himself tell us that is the very reason He came to this earth? He came to seek and to save the lost. He came not to call the righteous, but sinners to repentance. Does He not tell us that as the Good Shepherd, He would leave ninety-nine sheep in the fold and go after just one that was lost? *"For thus saith the Lord GOD; Behold, I, even I, will both search my sheep, and seek them out"* (Ezekiel 34:11).

And so the hand of God started events moving without either of us being aware of it. A certain preacher was coming to Scotland to conduct a crusade. I was vaguely interested. What was this man going to tell Scotland? I shelved my plan to run away for the time being.

In due time, I went with a bus from our church. For the first time in my life I found myself in a vast evangelical gathering. I had no idea what was going on. There I saw the words, "I am the Way, the Truth, and the Life", and I heard for the first time the words, "Ye must be born again." There was a new way of preaching from the Bible, very different from anything I had ever heard. My interest was truly aroused and questions were arising in my mind. Was there salvation outside the Church of Rome? The preacher said that salvation was obtained through believing in the finished work of Christ at Calvary, not through belonging to any particular church. All my training and indoctrination denied such a possibility. But this preacher kept asking us to repent and come to Christ for the forgiveness of sins. Who was right?

I forgot about running away. Repeatedly, I went back to hear the preacher, ten times in all. For the fourth time, I was seeking a way to peace with God. I did not receive Jesus Christ at any of the meetings for two main reasons: fear of my husband and the far greater fear of being involved with heretics. In spite of my fears, it now became the most important thing in my life to try to discover the truth. Nothing else mattered.

Gloriously Saved

Three months later, there was a follow-up to the crusade. Still seeking answers to all the questions that were troubling me, I attended the meetings in a near-by town. Night after night I went and the words of Psalm 107:6 became real for me, *"Then they cried unto the LORD in their trouble, and he delivered them out of their distresses."*

On Saturday my husband went away to fish for the day, and I went to the evening meeting. There, as the evangelist preached, I knew for certain that the Lord Jesus had settled the question of sin once and forever by His death, and that at Calvary the work of atonement had been finished. In believing in Jesus Christ and His finished work of salvation, my burden was lifted, my sins were forgiven. At last, the way to peace with God became a reality for me!

The evangelist spoke with me that night and told me to do two things: start reading the Bible every day and when I went home tell my husband that I was saved. Read the Bible and tell him! I didn't know which was worse! I was forty years old and the Bible had been the forbidden book which I had never opened in my life.

At midnight my husband arrived home. His train had been delayed and he was tired, cold and hungry. I met him at the door and told him I was saved. It most certainly was not the right moment. The next day I opened the Bible while my husband was at work and read a chapter of "begats" and I couldn't understand a word of it!

In the Wilderness

For three years, I was in a wilderness experience. My life had been completely changed; I knew where my duty lay as a wife. Yet, here I was a newly born Christian with no help or encouragement from minister, church or evangelical fellowship.

Then there was the opposition of my husband. He had no understanding of what had happened to me. Day by day I struggled on, continuing to read the Bible sticking mainly to parts of the New Testament which I could understand, and light came. *"Can God furnish a table in the wilderness?"* (Psalm 78:19).

Sometimes the terrible fear came upon me that perhaps I had taken the wrong step. However, the Lord led me to the sure and certain knowledge of the infallibility of His Word, *"which are able to make thee wise unto salvation through faith which is in Christ Jesus"* (2 Timothy 3:15). I hung onto the knowledge of the truth that had made me free. *"In all thy ways acknowledge him, and he shall direct thy paths"* (Proverbs 3:6).

The Fellowship of Believers

Through reading the word of God, there came the time when I desired to undergo believer's baptism. I did not know how to go about it, but seeing the name "Baptist Church" in the local paper, I went to a Sunday evening service when my husband was at work. Once inside I knew this was the place for me because the Word was being preached, the first preaching I had heard since the night I was converted three years earlier. The hand of fellowship was offered to me at the door for the first time in my life.

When my husband found out where I had been, he had other ideas. I was to attend the church where he was an elder. On this one point, I was determined I would not give in. Eventually I saw the minister of the church I was attending and asked to be baptized. The minister agreed to my request, but I would have to tell my husband and invite him to the service. The only thing I could think of saying was, "You tell him."

Home I went to tell my husband that a Baptist minister was coming to see him. The minister arrived and to my astonishment my husband sat and listened. For the first time he was challenged about salvation, challenged about the difference between being a member of a church and being a member of the body of Christ by new birth. The minister invited him to come and see me baptized and to my horror, he said he would.

The God Who Saves

The night for my baptism arrived. The first half of the service was conducted and the sermon preached. Baptism was not mentioned, rather the focus was on salvation. In the plan and purposes of God for each of our lives, His timing is always perfect. As I went under the water, symbolically into death with Christ, my husband believed and he was saved. My husband had passed from death to life; he had entered that church dead in sin and left it alive for ever more!

Knowing nothing of what happened, I dreaded the thought of going home on the bus with John. Like a typical Scot, he took his time before he told me what happened; but the following Sunday morning we were sitting together in that church, one in Christ.

Four weeks later he followed me through the waters of baptism. God saved both of us individually in His own appointed time. He saved our marriage, reconciled us to Himself, and to each other. Ours became a union truly made by God. Our marriage once on the rocks became firmly established on the Rock. "*And he led them forth by the right way, that they might go to a city of habitation*" (Psalm 107:7).

Peace at Last

Soon after my husband was converted, he lost his job and never worked again. A few months later, it was discovered that he had a fatal disease. In the month of February, 1971, John passed into the presence of his Lord. He has gone ahead to the city of habitation. "*He brought them out of darkness and the shadow of death, and broke their bands in sunder*" (Psalm 107:14).

God brought me out of fear and bondage into glorious freedom and the knowledge of how to "*worship Him in spirit and in truth*" (John 4:24). With the beggar in John's Gospel I also can say, "*One thing I know, that, whereas I was blind, now I see*" (John 9:25). I found God to be the God of the hopeless situation.

Is there anyone who has read this story and feels that his personal circumstances could not be worse, or has to struggle on in a divided house? Maybe someone has read this who thinks that everything necessary had been done to get to heaven by joining a church and being on a membership roll. To each one who reads this story, I would say, no matter how difficult your circumstances or how great your need, no matter what your problems are, you can discover even as I did, that God is the One who is able to deal with any situation, however hopeless. He is able to bring you into the glorious and satisfying life of peace which the world cannot give— peace with God.

"*Peace I leave with you, my peace I give unto you; ...Let not your heart be troubled, neither let it be afraid*" (John 14:27).

Sophia Tekien

And the Truth Made Me Free

Brought up in a strict Roman Catholic family where the emphasis was on God's punishment for sins, I was very much afraid of Him. From my early years, it was also impressed upon me that Jesus founded the Roman Catholic Church, that only in the Catholic Church was He actually present (body and blood) in Holy Communion and that "outside the Roman Church there was no salvation". I felt privileged indeed to have been born into the Catholic religion and wondered, "Why would anyone want to be anything else, since all other religions were founded by mere men?" Lest I defile myself, I would not even set foot into any of the Protestant churches.

God is Love

Although I became worldly minded as I matured, I legalistically tried to keep the commandments and to attend Mass regularly on Sundays and holy days. I even made numerous novenas. One novena consisted of taking the sacraments on nine consecutive first Fridays of the month and would help me get to heaven. I was also into astrology and leaned heavily on my horoscope readings concerning propitious days for my social activities. All in all, I considered myself to be a better than average Roman Catholic.

One day, while reading an autobiography of a convert to Catholicism, I was overwhelmed by his biblical references of God's love for us! God, Whom I so feared, was depicted as someone so loving, so caring. I fell in love with Him! I wanted nothing more than to know more about Him. Coupled with this knowledge of God's love for me was an awareness of my sinfulness. I had a distinct sense that Jesus could rescue me from a path leading to hell! I was horrified as I realized I was on my way to hell and did not even know it.

So awed was I with this revelation of God's love and forgiveness, I had no desire to continue in my old lifestyle. Worldly pursuits lost their appeal. I hungered to know more about God and the Bible. However, Bible classes in the Roman Catholic Church were non-existent; even reading the Bible was discouraged. The only place I thought would have such classes would be the convent. The mere idea repelled me.

Religious Life

After several months, when my unceasing desire to know God better through the Bible would not be stilled, I decided to check it out. Perhaps this was God's way of calling me to the religious life. I consoled myself with the idea that I would be with others who share my aspirations and that I could teach others via the Bible instead of the catechism as I was taught.

In my search to know from which of the hundreds of religious orders to choose, I had a dream which dispelled all doubts. In my dream I was in a simply furnished room with a crib and the Infant Jesus beside my bed. Although the windows were wide open, there was fresh fallen snow on the ground. I awakened feeling the dream was of significance. When I later browsed through some brochures on religious life, I noted that the Missionary Servants of the Most Blessed Trinity had an entrance date of August 5th, the feast of the Lady of the Snows. I felt God was answering my prayers by pointing to the exact place of His choice.

On the very next day, I boarded a train for Philadelphia, Pennsylvania. Although I was not fully acquainted with the work they did, that was unimportant. God's will was! If He wanted me in this place, nothing else mattered. When the Reverend Mother who interviewed me confirmed my interpretation of the dream, I needed to hear no more. Arrangements were made for me to enter. The conviction that life with the Missionary Servants of the Most Blessed Trinity was precisely God's will for me would sustain me during the thirty-one years I spent there. My faith was now inextricably interwoven with my vocation.

After a month in the community, I began to realize my hopes for Bible study would not materialize. We had readings of Scripture in our prayers but **no Bible study** *per se*. Although very disappointed, I could not leave. Whenever tempted to do so, I would remember the dream and the thought that would confront me was, "Why did I come, to please self or God?" There was a kind of peace in what I thought was His will for me.

My First Mission

During my first mission, God seemed to be trying to tell me something, but I was too prejudiced to hear or understand. While taking the parish census, I met quite a few Protestants living in the area. Contrary to what I had been led to believe, I found them to be exceptionally prayerful and godly people. What impressed me most about them was their personal love of Christ and their knowledge and love for the Bible. Mentioning this to the sisters, I was teased, "Who is going to convert whom?"

"August 1955 and I begin…"

Among some of these people, I met a Protestant minister who was a former Roman Catholic. He tried to explain to me what life was like for him and his family before he became a Christian, how despite daily Mass and sacraments, they knew nothing about God and the Bible. He also tried to explain that Jesus is only symbolically present in Holy Communion, but I wouldn't listen. Although deeply moved by his prayers for me before I left, I felt he made a terrible mistake leaving the Catholic Church which was founded by Christ Himself. After reading a booklet he gave me on the Gospel of John, I even returned to show him my Catholic belief in chapter six. In my ignorance of the Bible, I insisted our Lord **did** promise to give us His flesh to eat. In due time, the Lord would use this very chapter to open my eyes to the truth.

On another occasion, a Protestant patient whom I visited in a tuberculosis sanitorium asked me, "Sister, are you saved?" My reaction was, "Poor thing, none of us knows for sure we are saved until we die." According to Roman Catholic teaching, it is a sin of presumption to claim to know you are saved. Nevertheless, I could not help but think, "What wonderful Catholics these Protestants would make. They know their Bible and seem so close to God, so different from the Roman Catholic population who disdainfully regard sin as something they could simply confess tomorrow."

Since one of my incentives in entering religious life was to teach from the Bible, I had hoped the children in CCD classes could use a book with Bible stories. The priest, however, was not in accord with the suggestion. He was convinced that drilling the children with catechism answers was the only way.

Empty Efforts

In due time, despite my staunch Roman Catholic belief in the Real Presence in Holy Communion, I began to wonder if in fact one did get to know Jesus better through frequent reception of the sacraments. Year after year I saw no change in myself, nor in the sisters I lived with, nor in the children we taught in CCD classes. One priest tried to assure me that Jesus in Holy Communion would teach me all I needed to know about Him.

"I dared not even think of leaving"

In my attempts to grow spiritually by trying to tackle one fault at a time, I only succeeded in becoming depressed and needing professional help. One Roman Catholic psychologist advised me that I was a perfectionist with a scrupulous conscience and suggested I read Romans Chapter Seven. Without proper understanding of the Bible, I agreed I was probably was striving for the unattainable. The crux of the message, that only Jesus could accomplish in me what I was trying to do by my own efforts, eluded me.

Through the many years that followed, a brief sentence characterized my thinking, "Something is missing." Nevertheless, I dared not even think of leaving. That would be tantamount to turning my back on God.

The Word of Truth

Much of my dissatisfaction was alleviated when in 1972 I was introduced to the Charismatic Movement. While there was much emotionalism, I met people who were excited about the Bible and Jesus. Listening to their stories made me realize that God's call in my life was evident back in 1951. Later that call would find seed in His written Word and I would be quickened by the Holy Spirit. At these meetings, I began to learn what the Bible says about the need to born again and that when we are saved we are forgiven not only of our past sins, but present and future sins as well. As it says in Romans 8:1, *"There is, therefore, now no condemnation to them who are in Christ Jesus, who walk not after the flesh, but after the Spirit."* It was overwhelming to realize that I would never have to stand in judgment for any of my sins.

Through Christian friends, I also learned of the Family Radio program, an evangelical station which broadcasted Christ-centered music and biblically-oriented messages twenty-four hours a day, seven days a week. That station was such a tremendous blessing, I never changed my dial. I soon began to learn more about the Bible than I had in the previous twenty years. I hungered more than ever for a foundational understanding of God's Word. I longed for more time to just listen to this station. I would have been willing to do any mundane work if only I could tune in and hear more. I began to envy the laity who "on the outside" seemed to have more opportunities for Bible studies and group sharing than I had "on the inside".

Leaves of Absence

In 1977 during a crisis situation in one of my sister's lives, I asked for a leave of absence in order to be with her for awhile. The full reason, however, was twofold: I also needed time to evaluate my vocation.

I returned after nine months. My old conviction that the religious life was God's will for me was compounded by our religious community's Founder's Conferences on "Perseverance". A quote from one that struck me is, "Think, should you be tempted to leave here, where will you die? How will you die? How many will be lost because they are in the world?" With such admonitions in mind, I dared not leave. I was afraid I would loose my faith.

Although I accepted other assignments my heart was not in them. I found no satisfaction (as pastoral minister) in urging the fallen-away from the faith to come to Mass and receive the sacraments. I knew they and I needed to know more about God, the Bible, and His wonderful plan of salvation. What I was learning on Family Radio concerning salvation simply did not jive with the traditional teachings of the Roman Catholic Church.

In December of 1983 when I showed no enthusiasm about reassignment, I was told to ask for exclaustration, a leave of absence of up to three years, which would be permanent if I did not change. In as much as we were taught that the Superior's voice is the will of God, I was obedient. God was freeing me.

I started my leave of absence on January 19, 1984, and went to live with one of my sisters in Whiting, New Jersey. In God's providence, I had the opportunity to go to a place from which I heard many conferences on Family Radio. A missionary couple who lived next door brought me to America's Keswick. Here I heard wonderful, clear expositions of the Bible and pondered again my decades old question, "Which was the more important way to know God, the sacraments or the Bible?" The chaplain's response was a simply stated biblical truth, "The good thief was never baptized, yet was promised heaven that very day."

Disenchantment

During these daily Bible studies at Keswick's summer program, I heard something that had a pivotal effect on my life. Through reports given by missionaries on furlough I learned the godless state of life in France and Italy, both predominantly Roman Catholic countries. Neither of the countries knew much about the Bible, but could care less. When the missionary to Italy, a former Roman Catholic, told us that although Italy is ninety-five percent Roman Catholic only a few practice their religion, that it was home to the largest Communist Party in the world, I was flabbergasted. Was this not the center and heart of the Catholic Church? Were they not under the supervision of the very highest authority, the Pope?

As the missionary spoke of his own Roman Catholic training in grammar school, I could thoroughly relate to all that he said as it so completely matched my own experience. The teachings all focused on the Mass and the sacraments. There was nothing about the Bible or God's wonderful plan of salvation. "Why," I wondered, "is the Church so slow in imparting the most important truths of the Bible? Don't the bishops and priests realize that the brief Scripture readings during Mass are not enough?" It was the first time I perceived the Roman Catholic Church as a **mission field**. Nowhere was it evangelizing its people. I was heartsick.

Listening to these reports, I was torn in two. On the one hand, I was elated that many are now hearing more about God's Word in the Bible. Wasn't this my own reason for coming to Keswick? Could I not relate to previous emptiness? On the other hand there was deep sorrow, a sadness that the Catholic Church I was born into, the Church of my parents and their parents before them, the Church I loved and revered, was loosing ground. What grieved me most was that now many would not be receiving what I still believed was the actual body and blood of Jesus in Holy Communion. As I continued to wonder why the Church was so lax in teaching God's Word, one glaring fact was becoming more and more obvious: I was not alone in my disenchantment. The problem was universal.

Convicted by Truth

In the Fall, through a well-documented book entitled: *I Found the Ancient Way* written by a former priest, Manuel P. Vila, I was shocked to learn that the Roman Catholic Church deletes the Second Commandment from its teaching and divides the Tenth Commandment into two.

I immediately recalled the numerous times I had heard the Catholic Church being accused of idolatry because of its statues and my defensive response that we do not worship statues, but who they represent. What I didn't know was that the Second Commandment not only forbids worshiping and praying to statues, but even making them.

Since I was still of the belief that Jesus was actually present in the Eucharist, I decided to study the Corpus Christi Sunday Mass readings. I used the Jerusalem Bible edition and carefully researched all the footnotes and cross references. The Gospel reading for that Sunday was from Chapter Six of John, verses 51-58, where Jesus promises to give us His flesh to eat. Insight gained from this chapter practically forced me to leave the Roman Catholic Church. In the footnote for verses 51-58 was the following, "The Jews ask Jesus for a sign like that of the manna. Jesus tells them the Father's message which I pass on to man makes of Me man's true bread, a nourishment that only those with faith can receive. The Jews don't understand, only Peter and the apostles believe." It was added, "this doctrine is best understood in the light of Deuteronomy 8:3." Through the words "message" and "true bread", Deuteronomy 8:3 was clear to me: *"He humbled you, he made you feel hunger, he fed you with manna which neither you nor your fathers had known, to make you understand that man does not live on bread alone but that man lives on everything that comes from the mouth of Yahweh."* The verse and "the Word was made Flesh" came to mind; I realized that the Word is Jesus and Jesus, the Living Word in the Bible is the Father's Message! Christ reveals to us in human terms Who the Father is, and what the Father wants of us. Thus the Word made flesh is True Bread which through faith in His Word nourishes our souls. It is in hearing, reading, meditating, and munching on the Word of God that we are fed. By faith in true biblical teaching we have eternal life! *"So then, faith cometh by hearing, and hearing by the Word of God"* (Romans 10: 17).

So astonished was I to see in black and white what previously eluded me, I actually did not know what to believe. The sad fact is I was so dependent upon Roman Catholic authority for guidance that I initially could not trust myself or even God's Word when it contradicted the teachings of the Catholic Church.

As I continued to read the sixth chapter of John, the truth I had learned convicted me further. In verse 45 Jesus says, *"It is written in the prophets, And they shall all be taught of God. Every man, therefore, that hath heard, and hath learned of the Father, cometh unto me."* In verse 63 He explains, *"It is the Spirit that giveth life; the flesh profiteth nothing. The words that I speak unto you, they are spirit, and they are life."*

Peter and the apostles understood that our Lord was not referring to the eating of His physical body. Religious Jews, like Roman Catholics today, heard His teaching but did not understand. When teaching a parable about understanding the Word of God, Jesus said to His disciples, *"Unto you it is given to know the mysteries of the kingdom of God: but to others in parables; that seeing they might not see, and hearing they might not understand"* (Luke 8:10).

Upon being convicted of this truth, there was no way I could continue to go to Mass where Catholicism teaches the bread and wine are changed into the actual body and blood of Jesus. I also came to the conclusion that the worship of man-made bread as "God" during Mass is the height of idolatry.

A Disciple

Ironically, after floundering and languishing for more than thirty years, the Lord guided me back full circle to the very chapter

I refuted with the Protestant minister while on my first mission. John 8:31-32 explains the meaning of being a disciple, *"Then Jesus said to those Jews who believed on him, If ye continue in my word, then are ye my disciples indeed; And ye shall know the truth, and the truth shall make you free."*

I was indeed set free! The Lord continued to confirm this insight through many other passages in Scripture which deal with the eating of God's Word. Some of these Scriptures include Jeremiah 15:16, *"Thy words were found, and I did eat them;"* Job 23:12, *"I have esteemed the words of his mouth more than my necessary food;"* Psalm 119: 103, *"How sweet are thy words unto my taste! Yea, sweeter than honey to my mouth."*

"I was indeed set free"

Further, according to God's Word, the Bible, Old Testament sacrifices on which the Mass is based, were made obsolete by Christ's **once for all** sacrifice on the cross (Hebrews 10:9-10). *"But this man, after he had offered one sacrifice for sins forever, sat down on the right hand of God"* (Hebrews 10:12). *"Now where remission of these (sins) is, there is no more offering for sin"* (Hebrews 10:18).

Another belief I had to disown was purgatory. If people can get to heaven through their own sufferings and/or good works, then Jesus died on the cross in vain. Purgatory is the devil's ploy to make people think there will be a second chance.

A Personal Message

If you, dear reader, are a Roman Catholic, I urge you to turn to the Bible, and allow God Himself to be your teacher. It is only through God's Word that we get to know who He is and who we are in His sight. In order to understand the Bible, however, we need to be born again. It is not some Protestant minister, but Jesus Who tells us in John 3:3, *"Except a man be born again, he cannot see the kingdom of God."*

What Jesus is saying is that we must be born spiritually before we can understand His Word. *"But the natural man receiveth not the things of the Spirit of God; for they are foolishness unto him, neither can he know them, because they are spiritually discerned"* (1Corinthians 2:14). Being baptized with water, having religion, or basically being a good person does not save us. We must believe in Jesus Christ and what He has done for us in His death, burial and resurrection, and place our full trust in Him alone to be born again or saved. This means believing that when Jesus died a substitutionary death for us on the cross, He paid once for all the full penalty for all our sins, past, present and future. When we accept Jesus as our personal Savior, we receive new life, His life, and are sealed by the Holy Spirit as eternally belonging to Christ. **This** is the **Good News** of **God's Plan** of **Salvation**. It is in complete contrast to man's way of earning heaven by good works. Good works are the result of life in Christ, not the means of salvation or earning heaven. *"For by grace are ye saved through faith; and that not of yourselves: it is the gift of God: Not of works, lest any man should boast. For we are His workmanship, created in Christ Jesus unto good works, which God hath before ordained that we should walk in them"* (Ephesians 2: 8-10).

Purpose in Everything

While religious life was not the answer to satisfy the deep longings in my soul, I do not consider the thirty plus years in the convent totally wasted. In God's economy of time, nothing is wasted. There was a purpose. Perhaps it was the only way I could be convinced that I was not in a church founded by Christ. One aspect of my so-called vocation to the religious life that continued to puzzle me was the dream which so convinced me that I was in the precise place of God's choosing. Through a better understanding of Scripture and the wiles of the evil one, I have come to know that I was duped not by God, but by the deceiver himself, Satan. God's will is made known to us by and through His Word. Whatever cannot be confirmed by His Word, or is contrary to His Word, cannot be His will. None of the feasts that honor Mary are in the Bible or supported by Biblical truth. The Book of Revelation gives a severe warning about adding to or subtracting from God's Word. *"If any man shall add unto these things, God shall add unto him the plagues that are written in this book; And if any man shall take away from the words of the book of this prophecy, God shall take away his part from the tree of life"* (Rev. 22:18-19). Another warning that deals with all that is added to the true Gospel in the Catholic Church is in

Galatians, Chapter One. In verse one, Paul makes it clear that he is an apostle, *"not of men, neither by man, but by Jesus Christ, and God the Father who raised him from the dead."* Then in verse eight, Paul states, *"But though we, or an angel from heaven, preach any other gospel unto you than that which we have preached unto you, let him be accursed."*

My Current Position

I depend upon the Lord's promises to restore the years the locusts have eaten (Joel 2: 25). His generous care for me can never be outdone. I was released from my vows to serve God according to the Constitution of the Missionary Servants of the Most Blessed Trinity on May 21, 1985, freeing me to serve Him according to His Word. I no longer strive for perfection by my own efforts, but abide in the only One Who can make me perfect and acceptable to the Father by clothing me in His righteousness.

I do not espouse any particular denomination, I am simply a Bible-believing Christian who will never cease praising God for delivering me out the darkness of the Roman Catholic faith into the marvelous light of His truth. Knowing authority does not reside in Rome but in God's inerrant Word, I am assured of my salvation because it is Christ Who has accomplished it and offered it to me.

Freedom for You through Christ

If you, dear reader, are a Roman Catholic, I urge you to let the Word of God be your teacher. Consider the following passages:

Isaiah 64:6 *"All our righteousnesses are as filthy rags."*

Romans 3:10 *"There is none righteous, no not one."*

1 John 1:8 *"If we say that we have no sin, we deceive ourselves, and the truth is not in us."*

Romans 6: 23 *"For the wages of sin is death, but the gift of God is eternal life through Jesus Christ, our Lord."*

Hebrews 9:27 *"It is appointed unto men once to die, but after this the judgment."*

John 3:16 *"For God so loved the world, that he gave his only begotten Son, that whoever believeth in Him should not perish, but have everlasting life."*

John 1:12 *"But to as many as received Him, to them gave He power to become the children of God, even to them that believeth on His name."*

John 20:31 *"these* [Scriptures] *are written, that ye might believe that Jesus is the Christ, the Son of God, and that believing ye might have life through His name."*

His Word is Truth and the truth will make you free.

Donna Spader Shire
(formerly Sister Madonna Therese)

Mother's Vocation and God's Grace

Of the sixteen children born to my parents, two became priests and I became a nun. From earliest childhood we were taught that the Catholic Church was the only true church, and that in order to one day gain eternal life in heaven, we must be good and do good. My mother's greatest desire was to have at least one of her daughters dedicated to be a nun. I was chosen to be that daughter. I attended parochial high school and, immediately following graduation in 1960, entered the convent of the School Sisters of St. Francis in Milwaukee, Wisconsin.

Life in the convent was severe and strict. We were taught about the saints of the church and Church doctrine, but not the Scriptures. I received my first Bible after ten years in the convent. It was not put into my hands by the Catholic Church, but by a group of Charismatics.

My Brother Shares

My younger brother had come to know the Lord through Campus Crusade. He had left engineering school and was attending Moody Bible Institute. He came to visit me often and shared his new-found faith. Through Ephesians 2:8-9 he tried to convince me that salvation is a free gift which can only be obtained by trusting Christ alone and that our good deeds do not save us, as is stated so clearly in Scripture, *"not by works of righteousness which we have done, but according to His mercy he has saved us"* (Titus 3:5). It was obvious that my brother had the assurance of eternal life that I so

119

desperately desired, but I could not believe that my church had misled me in such an important issue.

The Convent and Empty Religion

For five years I searched to find peace and happiness on my own. I tried yoga, transcendental meditation, Silva mind control, tongues and prophesying. Each seemed to satisfy for a time, but in the end, left a spiritual void. After fifteen years in the convent, and still not finding the peace with God for which I had longed, I began seriously to question my life as a religious. I had entered the convent believing that there I could be "good" enough. However, I found that even in a convent the sisters sin just as women do in the world.

Change of Habits

In 1975 I wrote to the Pope and received his permission to be released from my vows. In leaving the convent I felt as though I had failed myself, my family, and my Church. Rather than returning home, I went East to live with a friend who was also an ex-nun. The two of us chose to make up for all our years of cloistered life by trying everything that the world had to offer. It did not take long to see that the worldly life has nothing to offer either.

Direct Prayer

One evening when I returned to our apartment, I found my friend in real trouble. She had been drinking and smoking marijuana and was in a rage. She seemed to want to end her life completely. I became frightened, the more I tried to calm her down, the violent and angry she became. Finally, in desperation, I grabbed her and began praying. I believe that this was the first time I had ever prayed directly to God, bypassing the Blessed Mother and the Saints. In doing so, God heard my prayer and immediately she calmed down.

Amazing Grace

We decided that night to find out the truth about God. We knelt down and sincerely asked Him for help and forgiveness. We asked Him to straighten out the mess that we had made of our lives, for like Isaiah, we saw that our righteousness was as filthy rags. We were not familiar with terms such as "saved" and "born again", but from that moment I began to experience for the first time in my life His peace "that passes understanding". From that time on there was an obvious change in my heart and life. The Word of God became a light unto my path, where before it had been confusing. Verses took on new meaning, *"In whom we have redemption through His blood, the forgiveness of sins, according to the riches of his grace"* (Ephesians 1:7). *"But God commendeth His own love toward us, in that while we were yet sinners, Christ died for us"*, *"For if when we were enemies we were reconciled to God by the death of His Son, much more, being reconciled, we shall be saved by His life"* (Romans 5:8, 10).

Since my conversion to Jesus Christ, God has blessed me in many ways. I attended a Bible school in England where I received very sound doctrinal teaching. I was given a trip to the Holy Land, where I had the joy of walking where my Lord walked centuries ago and where I received a better perspective of Scripture. I have been a counselor with a family agency, have married (a widowed man), and am not only a wife, but a mother of five and a grandmother of ten.

Each day, whether in good or difficult circumstance, like Isaiah, I can say, *"I will greatly rejoice in the Lord, my soul shall be joyful in my God; for He hath clothed me with the garments of salvation, He hath covered me with the robe of righteousness, as a bridegroom decketh himself with ornaments, and as a bride adorneth herself with her jewels"* (Isaiah 61:10).

Perhaps you, too, have concluded that a religious life can not earn salvation. If you want to know Jesus Christ as your personal Savior, believe in Him and His death, burial and resurrection which paid your sin debt in full and receive the gift of salvation that He freely offers by grace through faith. *"And we know that the Son of God is come, and hath given us an understanding, that we may know Him that is true, and we are in Him that is true, even in His Son Jesus Christ. This is the true God, and eternal life. Little children, keep yourselves from idols. Amen"* (1 John 5:20-21).

Know that eternal life is in Christ and Him alone; looking to and praying to all others is idolatry. Obey God's warning in Scripture, *"Beware lest any man spoil you through philosophy and vain deceit, after the tradition of men, after the rudiments of the world, and not after Christ. For in Him dwelleth all the fullness of the Godhead bodily. And ye are complete in Him, which is the Head of all principality and power"* (Colossians 2:8-10).

He is waiting for you to trust Him, that indeed in Him you are complete! Do it now, you will forever thank Him!

Lucille Poulin

The Truth Shall Make You Free!

My testimony is written with the compassion of our Lord and Savior Jesus Christ for His glory and to present the knowledge of salvation to those who read it. *"To give light to them that sit in darkness and in the shadow of death, to guide our feet into the way of peace"* (Luke 1:79).

It is my story of fifty years as a Roman Catholic, thirty-five of these years as a nun before I came to know and receive the gift of eternal life, avoiding eternal damnation and entering into the joy of the Lord. I live now led by the Spirit, delighted to do the will of my Father and looking forward to hearing from the King Himself, "Well done, good and faithful servant."

After thirty-one years of total dedication to religious life as a nun among the Sisters of Charity of Notre Dame d'Evron, nursing the sick and comforting the dying, I had come to utter despair. Though generally loved, approved and applauded within the medico-religious world, enjoying remarkable success, I was on the brink of self-destruction and overwhelmed by the fear of hell. The void in my heart and the inability to stop sinning had overthrown my iron-hard determination to be faithful forever. Faithful to what? to whom? and why? There was such mystery and frightening uncertainties concerning the hereafter.

Roman Catholic Roots

Born in Vegreville in 1924, I was raised in a staunch Roman Catholic family. Endowed with an energetic, daring character, a quick, inquisitive and credulous mind and a generous heart, I got in more predicaments than all my peers put together. Rebellious and vicious streaks soon received their just reward: one heavy unusual whipping subdued those particular lopsided priorities for many years. However, I developed an ongoing fear of impending punishment.

Following the traditions of my fathers, I had learned to obey, as every good Catholic does without question or query, all the religious leaders with an extreme reverence and awe toward the pope, the holy father, the sovereign pontiff. Forbidden to read the Bible lest we be led astray, we were left at the mercy of hirelings, the false prophets of our day. Instructed that the voice of the superiors expressed the will of God, we were expected to obey "blindly".

A "High" Calling

At the age of fourteen, I heard a priest tell our class about Jesus who died for us. He showed us a colored picture of a man crowned with thorns, hands tied, head bowed and blood dripping from his brow. "Now, each one of you," he said, "will have to pay back this tremendous lover, and the surest and quickest way to do so is to become a priest or nun, since it is a form of martyrdom." "Some are too passionate," he added, "and will have to marry. It will be very difficult for them to get to heaven, yet possible through much penance, sacrifices and sufferings. All of us, of course, will pass through purgatory, for who can be perfect and holy enough to go straight to heaven?"

As I stared at the picture, resounding deep within me was, "He died for me!" I set out then and there to pay back this tremendous lover, whatever the cost! I would be a nun, atone quickly for my sins through self-denial and penance and then become a great saint. Forsaking the secret desire to become a spouse and a mother later on, I entered the convent at age fifteen. Following two difficult years of training, I vowed my life to an 'unknown god'. At age seventeen, I was a full-fledged nun believing with all my heart that I pleased Jesus. That same day, a prominent Superior spoke an awesome prediction upon me, "Poor little girl, you will be so very unfaithful to your most holy vocation." This brought my "home-made" tower of holiness to a crash. "God" had spoken. Fear and sorrow gripped me and I was crushed.

Deception and Hypocrisy

However, well-fitted with a mystified yoke of bondage and the mask of hypocrisy, sincere but deceived, I set out to pray hard, to work hard, and to try hard to be a really holy nun anyway. Surely, I thought, nothing could be too hard to please Jesus. Now I know that it was a zeal for God, but not according to knowledge. Ignorant of God's righteousness, I was going about establishing my own righteousness which is as filthy rags before the Living God (Isaiah 64:6). Little did I know that Roman Catholicism preaches "another Jesus", "another gospel", and has received and gives "another spirit" (Galatians 1: 6-8, 2 Corinthians 11:4).

God said, *"My people are destroyed for lack of knowledge"* (Hosea 4:6). Woe to the false shepherds who make this people trust a lie, who preach salvation by human merit instead of the finished work of Jesus Christ on the cross (John 19:30, Romans 10:4).

Retreat from Reality

Though bewildered by many things, I was relatively happy, delighting in my great deeds for God. At the age of twenty-three, what I feared came upon me. I fell in love with a handsome twenty-four year old medical doctor. Tearing myself away from a deep mutual love, I bluntly refused his marriage proposal and with-drew into my phantom world with heartache and a tormented soul. Overwhelmed with hurt, guilt and shame, another struggle began: uncon-trollable wild fantasies with prince charming, even long after he departed from the hospital. A nun loving a man!

"Establishing my own righteousness, age seventeen"

My shame lasted for some twenty-five years. Psychological, medi-cal, psychiatric and religious counseling was useless. Yet, I remained determined to be faithful unto death. Within my inner being flickered a secret hope that someday, someone would be able to tell me all about Jesus who cares, is alive and able to help in time of need.

Concealed under the appearance of a holy, sincere and lovable nun, festered self-righteousness, seducing spirits, lies in hypocrisy and doctrines of devils (1 Timothy 4:1-3). Deep-seated anger was rising slowly within as I witnessed so many subtle disorders, not only in myself but also in the religious world around me. We all seemed unable to help one another effectively. Often condemna-tion, hurt, and hate prevailed. Nevertheless, I continued to serve the sick with all the human compassion I could muster. For twenty-one years, each year I would yearn for those ten days of retreat, intermission between three hundred fifty-five days of long working hours. During these retreats, I would drain every religious counselor available, only to be spurred on to a greater devotion to the sacraments, Mary worship (as mediatrix of all graces), and blind obedience to my 'holy' constitutions and to 'holy' Mother Church. This only increased the heaviness of my heart for, year after year, had I not tried as hard as I could? However, I would go back to hard labor with a greater fear of failure and possible eternity in hell. Nervousness and sickness soon made life unbearable.

Deadly Ignorance

Almost overnight I appeared as a dangerous nun. I began to question the entire religious system, demanding concrete answers which never came. Unknowingly, I had become a threat to our morbid security. Yet, all I wanted was to stop sinning and live holy. I wanted some improvement in my life and peace of heart, mind and soul concerning judgement and eternity. Far from me was the thought that so many well-educated, proper nuns, priests, bishops and popes, and so many fine Catholic people could be so "deadly" wrong.

Still fumbling in the utter darkness of false doctrines, I wrote to Pope Paul VI sincerely believing he could and would rescue the least of his flock. A nebulous answer from one of his helpers suggested the annulment of my vows of poverty (never any personal possessions), chastity (never love a man or marry) and obedience (obey every Superior). The letter suggested that I search elsewhere if not satisfied. This brought me to ultimate hopelessness. Never having heard the message of salvation, I was under the curse of the law and therefore headed for death and destruction. Ignorance certainly was not bliss, *"There is a way which seems right unto man, but the end thereof are the ways of death"* (Proverbs 14:12).

God Heard My Cry

Though thoroughly confused, I still believed what I had been taught: outside the Catholic Church there is no salvation. Where could I possibly go? Fear of hell gripped me by day and by night. Shortly after receiving the papal letter, alone in my convent room one night in 1972, I was on the brink of self-destruction. A desperate cry rose up within me, "If there is a living God in heaven, have mercy on me a sinner!"

At last, I had become honest enough to receive God's answer for life, regardless of the cost or what anyone would say. Exhausted and helpless, I fell to the floor unable to move for hours. Within a few days, God sent a woman who brought me to a gospel meeting where I heard the truth,

"Except ye repent, ye shall all likewise perish." (Luke 13:3)

"By grace are ye saved through faith and not of yourselves, it is a gift of God; not of works, lest any man should boast." (Ephesians 2: 8-9)

"The wages of sin is death but the gift of God is eternal life through Jesus Christ, Our Lord." (Romans 6: 23)

"Ye shall know the truth and the truth shall make you free." (John 8: 32)

"Jesus Christ...loved us, and washed us from our sins in his own blood." (Revelation 1:5)

In my nun's garb in a huge Protestant hall kneeling among other sinners at the altar of repentance, I wept with godly sorrow at the Savior's feet. For the first time, I really believed that God had forgiven all my sins. I received Jesus Christ as my Lord and Savior. Fear of damnation and heaviness lifted and I knew the joy of being forgiven by the Almighty and Living God. Peace flowed within me like a mighty river. I was born again by the incorruptible seed of the Word of God which abides forever (1 Peter 1:23).

Newborn Zeal

Back to the nunnery with the exuberance of a newly born creature and lacking wisdom as a babe, I cornered every nun to tell her my sins had been forgiven, that Jesus lived in me and I loved her so much, proclaiming "It's free, it's free for you, too, sister!" A prominent Superior sympathetically suggested that I see a psychiatrist. This hurt me deeply and I refused. In spite of frequent reprimands for such unusual behavior, I wanted everyone to be saved and experience the joy of the Lord, now!

An Impossible Mix

For about four years, I continued the best I knew how to try to blend light with darkness, truth with error, the principles of the truth of Christ with Romanism. Finally, after much useless struggle, I realized there can be no compromise with truth. Later, I saw clearly how believers make shipwreck of their faith by mixing truth and error. God will not be mocked.

Nevertheless, at that time, it seemed impossible for me to leave the convent and Catholicism. Had I not been born a Catholic? Shouldn't one stay and help them? These are the usual lies of Satan to all religious people just before they emerge into the liberty of the children of God. Having been involved with Charismatics, I discerned a counterfeit of the work of the Holy Spirit. As my knowledge of God's Word increased, I understood that I was not to be ashamed of the Gospel of Jesus Christ, *"for it is the power of God unto salvation to everyone that believes"* (Romans 1: 16). Thus, I simply left the teachings of man's wisdom to do it God's way. It was a matter of putting away "salvation by attainment" by human merit to receive "salvation by atonement" by divine mercy. In the joy of personal relationship with Christ, I had begun to walk by His Spirit (Galatians 5:16).

No Easy Road

The road of freedom was rugged and steep. It took determination to live willingly in obedience to God's truth. Whosoever will (Revelation 22:17)! God is faithful and by His grace I was able to forsake the vain religion received from my ancestors through tradition. The most difficult chain to break was the Eucharist, Catholic communion. While reading John, Chapter Six, I received understanding about the Lord's supper. *"It is the Spirit that gives life, the flesh profits nothing. The words that I speak to you, they are spirit and they are life, but there are some of you that believe not"* (vs. 63-64).

By the grace of God, I walked away from all religious and social systems. It meant the forsaking of precious friendships, even my own relatives, many of whom turned against me like ravenous wolves. In obedience, I pursued peace with all men (Hebrews 12:14) and sought to separate myself from everything that did not line up with the Word of God in order to live as a daughter of my Father in heaven (2 Corinthians 6:17-18). Therefore, rather than simply walking away from the idolatrous practices of the religious order, I choose to request a release from my vows from the religious authorities. The reply from the Superior General was, "Dear Sister Martha, we really do not understand what is happening to you, but we dare not stand against the work of the Holy Spirit. Therefore, we release you today to a new calling of God upon your life. Expect persecutions as you enter so deep an involvement with the Lord's work." With tears of joy and thanksgiving to God for such a mighty liberation, I embraced Mother Odette, expressing gratitude for her painstaking tolerance and the many humane attitudes of other nuns during my long years of struggle for freedom and peace of mind and heart. These happenings appeared to me as a flight for refuge to lay hold of the hope set before me, the sure and steadfast anchor of my soul (Hebrews 6:19). I knew Jesus Christ had delivered me from a lifetime of bondage and fear of death (Hebrews 2:15). I was free, for the Son had set me free!

Another work of grace was the overcoming of anger and indignation against the leaders of Romanism who would persistently refuse the message of God's precious salvation, preferring to go to their destruction along with a throng of precious but deceived Catholics. I had entered God's rest and was now tasting the liberty of the children of God. Sanctified by truth, freed from sin, I became the servant of righteousness, choosing to walk according to God's Word rather than according to what the world, religion, circumstances or the devil says (Galatians 5:13). I pray for my persecutors, forgiving them as Christ forgives (Luke 23: 34) and do good to those who hate me (Romans 12: 17). Problems arise more than ever, but they are solved through Jesus Christ who causes me to triumph in all things. How delightful it is to have no more fear, but the power of the Spirit enabling me to have a sound mind and to love. That is true freedom!

A Ministry of Reconciliation

While in the ministry of reconciliation (2 Corinthians 5: 18), I ushered my ninety-six year old mother out of a senior home into private home life with me. For two years we thrived together, enjoying divine health as we grew in knowledge and grace. While continuing to care for my aging mother, the Lord called me to serve my niece, her young family (five children under age nine) and her husband, Daniel. During the next few years, the Holy Spirit dealt with Daniel bringing him to a knowledge of his sinfulness and by grace he was saved through faith. My niece had six more children and the older two made decisions to believe in the Lord Jesus Christ. Assisting with bringing up children according to God's perfect plan meant the adults involved followed a consistency of discipline and compassion while training each child the way he should go. The children were taught to work in the world but not be of the world. This ministry of love, joy and peace became a witness to the truth that where the Spirit of the Lord is there is liberty.

He is Able

How can I be so sure of myself? Because I am sure of Him in Whom I have believed and I am persuaded that He is able to keep that which I have committed to Him against that day (Jude 24). I

am in love with the God-man, Christ Jesus and about my Father's business, laboring in His vineyard. The fields are white and it is harvest time. I live for the precious moment of His coming, Jesus Christ, *"in whom we have redemption through his Blood, even the forgiveness of sins"* (Colossians 1:14). It is a matter of being a doer of the Word (James 1:22) for

"Now, as I am in the Lord secure"

I know who I am in Christ Jesus. I have been sealed in the Holy Spirit of promise and dare not forget what Peter said to believers when he warned them not to forget that they were purged from their old sins, *"giving all diligence, add to your faith virtue; and to virtue, knowledge; and to knowledge, self-control; and to self-control, patience; and to patience, godliness; and to godliness, brotherly kindness, love...to make your calling and election sure; for if you do these things ye shall never fall"* (2 Peter 1:5-11). Living as the Lord directs, it is possible to be faithful servants.

Believers are to hold fast to that which is given to us by God so as not to lose the opportunity to glorify the Lord. We serve to receive an imperishable crown (1Corinthians 9:25). Those who have a fearful heart, who have grown weary in the narrow way, can be encouraged by the Word of the Lord, "Be strong! Fear not!" Backsliders, slide back quickly into the arms of our Savior, let Him be your victory over all that draws you away from Him.

Precious people who are so tired of sinning, of being sick and bitter, weary of Satan's tyranny, come to Jesus. He will give you rest. Repent and be converted that your sins may be blotted out. Hear the Savior's plea, *"Come out of her my people* [out of the great Babylon, social and religious] *that ye may be not partakers of her sins and that ye receive not of her plagues"* (Revelation 18:14). *"O taste and see that the Lord is good; blessed is the man that trusteth in Him"* (Psalm 34:8).

The things that are impossible with man are possible with God! Salvation is available to all who believe in the finished work of Jesus Christ on the cross, that He died, was buried and rose again

(1 Corinthians 15:3-4). He who knew no sin became sin for us and took upon Himself the penalty of our sin, which is death. He who loved us and washed us from our sins in His own blood has made us kings and priests unto God the Father. To Him be glory and dominion forever and ever. Amen.

> *"I waited patiently for the Lord: and He inclined unto me and heard my cry.*
>
> *He brought me up also out of an horrible pit, out of the miry clay and set my feet upon a rock and established my goings.*
>
> *And he hath put a new song in my mouth even praise unto our God. Many shall see it and fear and shall trust in the Lord!"* (Psalm 40:1-3).

Doreen Eberhardt (D'Antonio)

This Is My Story

"There is a way which seemeth right unto a man, but the end thereof are the ways of death." Proverbs 14:12

My Desire to Serve God

I was born and raised in a Catholic family. My mother was very devout. The point came in my life when I wanted to serve God in a special way. Since I was a Catholic, the only way I knew was to enter the convent. I decided to enter the Sisters of Christian Charity. This particular Order attracted me because of their friendliness, congeniality and charitableness. Here I thought I would be happy and serve the Lord the way He wanted me to serve Him. From the moment I entered, I was told that I did not deserve this "Holy Vocation" and that I would not last long if I did not measure up to all their standards. I determined to make a good Sister of Christian Charity. However, it did not take me long to find out the truth about convent life. Instead of peace, harmony and working together, I found contention, backbiting, arguing and much unpleasantness and uneasiness in the atmosphere.

A False System of Works

While in the convent, I was preparing to be a teacher. Every day we had instructions on how to be a good and effective sister, and then we had a second lesson on Catholic doctrines such as the Mass, sacraments, rosary, infallibility of the Pope, etc. These doctrines began to seem empty to me, like a complicated system of works, sacrifices, and penances which you gathered together, hoping you would get to heaven faster, but with no **real** assurance of whether or not you will make it to heaven as soon as you die. I diligently started praying to God to increase my faith so that I would not doubt the teachings of the Catholic Church. However, I remained in this state for a number of years, just continuing on day by day no matter how hard things were. I still thought I could earn my salvation, but this is not so, as we read in Ephesians 2: 8-9, *"For by grace are ye saved through faith; and that not of yourselves: it is the gift of God: Not of works, lest any man should boast."*

In the convent we are kept very busy so that we would not have enough time to think about the falseness of the system. The rising bell rang at 5:30 A.M. followed by an hour and a half in chapel of formalized prayer, the Mass, then chores, college classes, meditation and rosary. Everyone was brainwashed to the ideas of the Roman Catholic Church, such as prayers to Mary, asking her to intercede to God for us and calling her the "Mother of God". We also faithfully wore scapulars to help us by-pass purgatory.

Driven by Fear

You are not allowed to tell your family or friends what really happens inside the convent. Everything was to be presented as a rosy picture, and all suffering, pain, illnesses and unhappiness kept inside yourself. You are robotized to think, act, talk and do the same thing, all at the same time. It is the aspect of **fear** that keeps girls in the convent, fear of leaving the "one true Church", as the Catholics like to say, and possibly risking your chance to get to heaven. You are never taught to ask Christ for help or to give thanks to Him. It is always pray to Mary, Joseph, or some other "Saint" such as Anthony, Jude, etc. There is much superstition found in the convent. For example, they would place a statue of St. Joseph on the window ledge so that it would not rain, but it still rained. They kept a statue of Mary on the dishwasher so that it would continue to work, but it still broke down. In the Bible, Deuteronomy 16:22, we read, *"Neither shalt thou set thee up any image; which the Lord thy God hateth."* And in Exodus 20:4, *"Thou shalt not make unto thee any graven image, or any likeness of any thing that is in heaven above, or that is in the earth beneath, or that is in the water under the earth."* Can you imagine such pagan superstition in the twentieth century?

Tradition Over Truth

The rosary never answered any of my prayers, as it supposedly did for the others. Praise God, today I understand why. Matthew 6:7, *"But when ye pray, use not vain repetitions, as the heathen do: for they think that they shall be heard for their much speaking."* Confession never gave me that washed clean feeling as it did for the others. Now I see why. It says in Romans 14:12, *"every one of us shall give account of himself to God."* We are accountable directly to God, **not to a priest**, for our sins. Praise God for His mercy, by giving me doubt, during those convent years. Receiving the "host" at Mass, the supposed body and blood of Christ, as we were taught, never helped strengthen my faith. It was just a dry piece of wafer to me. There was nothing to hold on to that was real. Colossians 2:8 warns us, *"Beware lest any man spoil you through philosophy and vain deceit, after the tradition of men, after the rudiments of the world, and not after Christ."* But Roman Catholics still insist that their tradition is better than God's Word. As the years rolled on, I continued in my unrepentant state before God, for I had not yet come to see that salvation is only through Christ.

Answered Prayer

In January of 1972, I began to come to an awakening of the truth. I prayed and asked God whether or not I should stay in the convent. God showed me that I should leave and He blessed me for the first time in all those years with peace in my heart and a happy and relaxed state of mind. When I told my superior of my decision, I was told that I was emotionally upset and not to make such a serious decision for at least another three or four months. I was told that my parents would no longer love me if I left, and that I would not command respect if I did not wear the habit of the sisters. But I kept praying that God would release me from there. I did not know that my parents had both been saved and were praying for God to take me out of the convent. They did not want a divided household, and prayed that their only children (both in the religious life) would also be saved by God's infinite mercy. They believed in Acts 16:31, *"Believe on the Lord Jesus Christ, and thou shalt be saved."* After many days of prayer, my Superior finally told me that if it was really what I wanted, I could leave.

Salvation by Believing in Jesus Christ

I left the convent February 1, 1972. When I came home, I was in such a confused state that I cried over any little thing. I totally turned against God. I did not want to hear anything about religion. I felt that my world was shattered and I was fearful of the outside world. My parents had been saved under the ministry of Rev. Alex Dunlap on January 17, 1972. They continued to live their new Christian lives as they did before I came home. They encouraged me to go to church with them, so I would go to their church (Cedar Grove Church, a fundamental Bible preaching church), but only to be polite and not cause friction in the house. My mother would listen to Oliver B. Green and his Bible study in the morning, and I would listen to be polite.

Finally, through the deep concerns and many prayers of the Christians at my parents' church, I came, six weeks later, to see that I was a sinner. Without Christ's precious blood, which was shed on the cross for me, I would surely go to eternal damnation, if I did not believe in Jesus Christ as my all-sufficient Lord and Savior. I have let Christ rule my life, I have received Him into my heart and He has saved me from my sins. Now I know, that when I die, I will go straight to heaven and be with my Lord and Savior Jesus Christ.

A Final Message

Now that you have read this story of how Christ saved me, I pray that you, too, will recognize your sinful condition, *"For all have sinned, and come short of the glory of God"* (Romans 3:23) and receive Jesus Christ as your Savior.

"With my brother, Frank, who was in the seminary"

I praise the Lord that He has saved my whole family. My brother, Frank, who was studying for the priesthood now preaches the Word of God rather than the traditions of man. He has realized through the Bible in I Timothy 2:5 that *"there is one God, and one mediator between God and men, the man Christ*

136

Jesus." This one mediator is not the Roman Catholic priest, as Catholic doctrine teaches.

If any parent reading this testimony has a daughter or son in the religious life, I **plead** with you to take them out of that system. Do you ever think seriously about where you will spend eternity? There are only two places: heaven through Christ or hell by Catholicism and its works. I am sure you have all received gifts from family and friends, and you graciously accepted the gift with pleasure and happiness. God is also **freely** offering you the gift of eternal life, *"...the gift of God is eternal life through Jesus Christ our Lord"* (Romans 6:23). *"For God so loved the world, that he gave his only begotten Son, that whosoever believeth in him should not perish, but have ever-lasting life"* (John 3:16).

"Behold, now is the accepted time; behold, now is the day of salvation" (II Corinthians 6:2). Accept Jesus Christ, your gift of salvation, **now**. He is the only way. *"I am the way, the truth, and the life: no man cometh unto the Father, but by me"* (John 14:6).

"Serving the Lord using ventriloquism"

After five and a half years in the convent, I am now serving my precious Lord and Savior as a missionary through the Gospel Outreach, Inc., P. O. Box 905, Taylors, SC 29687-0905. Please feel free to contact me if at any time you have questions or would like additional information.

16

Eileen M. Doran

A Labyrinthian Way

Each life comes fresh from the hand of God and winds its way along a totally unique path from beginning to end. Mine certainly is no different from the myriad lives that have come and gone through the ages. I was born into an Irish Catholic family, the third generation removed from the days of the potato famine immigration. My Mom, however, hailed back to revolutionary days in her French heritage and had been raised in Baptist and Methodist churches until she married my father and converted to Catholicism on making that commitment.

Catholic Education

Except for occasional attendance with my parents at church, my introduction to God came when I began to attend a Catholic school in Jersey City, New Jersey, as a first grader. (I only remember one lay teacher, a lovely young woman with an artificial leg, who taught me in the third grade.)

My first grade teacher was a kindly and saintly older woman clothed in the garb of the religious order to which she belonged. I treasured the brief moments when Sister Angelita would place me on her lap and express her motherly affection. As I learned of Jesus and of His death on the cross, I determined to give my life to Him, too, as a member of the same religious order. Throughout the years of grammar school I ardently participated in the various religious activities presented to me as pleasing to the God I was coming to know and longed to serve as completely and purely as possible.

Several times I made the "nine first Fridays" wondering how God would figure out all the plenary indulgences credited to my account. Ejaculations (a one phrase prayer) were generally worth hundreds of days' indulgence. An advent prayer said every day of advent carried a plenary indulgence. I began to go to Mass daily in the seventh grade. I attended novenas to Mary and to Saint Francis Xavier. I prayed to Saint Christopher for travel, Saint Anthony for lost articles, and Saint Jude for hopeless cases.

Convent Preparation

During the seventh grade, a young woman came to our school to speak of the preparatory high school conducted by the religious order stationed in our school. My desire to serve God found immediate application as she explained that this school accepted girls after graduating from the eighth grade.

My Dad was duly proud of me and spoke so to his still deeply Irish Catholic family. There had not been a "vocation" since an aunt of theirs had become a nun somewhere in Pennsylvania.

The four years of high school passed quickly as I pursued a regimen of strong academics coupled with a rigorous schedule of prayer and religious studies. Among the spiritual experiences of those years, two in particular stand out. When we were faced with the possibility or actuality of inclement weather, we interceded via Mary by singing a beautiful Gregorian chant of her "Magnificat". If the sun came beaming into the room we, of course, credited her with this event. In another Marian devotion, we recited the rosary beads each noon after lunch. I found a book called Rosary Novenas, which contained meditations on the fifteen mysteries of the rosary and took the monotony out of the recitation of ten "Hail Mary's" per mystery. We recited them, five mysteries at a time, grouped as the joyful, sorrowful, and glorious mysteries of the rosary. The life, death and resurrection of Jesus were focused on the "Blessed Virgin Mary".

During these years I actually dedicated myself to Jesus through Mary after reading books about Saint Louis DeMontford who advocated this method of intercession. Jesus was said to be too unapproachable for us. Mary was more on our level as imperfect human beings. Yet she was said to have been conceived free from "original sin" and to have lived a perfect life. Nevertheless, her model was seen to be more valid than that of Jesus for the purpose of our emulation. She was billed as the "co-redemptrix" along with Jesus. After all, she was present at the foot of the cross when Jesus died.

Religious Formation

Upon graduation from preparatory school, I was accepted into the postulancy of the Sisters of Charity of Saint Elizabeth at Convent Station, New Jersey. I spent a blissful year studying freshman college courses and waiting on tables of college girls for their meals.

During the following year I became **a novice**. This was a cloistered year of preparation for formal entrance into the community by the taking of the vows of poverty, chastity and obedience. Only studies of religion and religious music were permitted along with various chores in the motherhouse. Silence was observed except for recreation periods, one hour each in the afternoon and evening and on special occasions as granted by the superior. The philosophy of the Mistress, the woman put in charge of the forty-five of us, was to break any self will that might arise in each of us during that year. She did this by almost daily accusation of faults, some real, but most imaginary, to each of us both in public and privately. Humiliation was the tool for training in sanctification. On one occasion I received "public penance" and had to recite the Fifty-first Psalm kneeling in front of the assembled group after night prayers. Keeping the rules perfectly was the answer to becoming perfect. Penance erased any imperfection. It was a higher form of sanctification than a lay person could attain. But the method of training precluded any hope for the actual attainment of the goal.

By the end of the year I was convinced I would never make "sainthood". Sister Patricia emulated the few who had had "conversions". Although I prayed as long and as fervently as I knew how, and tried to look as holy as might be pleasing to her, I left the novitiate convinced something was basically wrong with me. The mistress had said she would admit me to vows but that I would never become a good religious. I felt even God could not approve of me. But I still believed this was the best way to serve God. I knew of no other way to serve God unreservedly. So I took my vows of poverty, chastity and obedience at the end of that year. Now I was to live up to the motto of the congregation, "Who lives to the rule, lives to God." Despite the gnawing discouragement eating at my soul, I purposed to serve God as best I knew how. That was all I could possibly attain.

Life as a Nun

After two additional years of college studies on the mother-house grounds, I was awarded a Bachelor of Science degree from the College of Saint Elizabeth. This was followed by an assignment to teach biology in a diocesan high school. During the summers I pursued a Masters Degree at Catholic University in Washington, D.C. During the school years, along with a normal teaching load, including the monitoring of extra-curricular activities, I obtained federal grants for additional studies related to my teaching, attending local colleges and universities on a part-time basis.

Life was more than busy and I began to regain some of my lost self-worth. At one point, I was asked by a priest stationed at the high school to team-teach a drug curriculum with him. We became friendly, but I was totally unprepared for his leading into a more than friendship status. After dinner together in a restaurant one evening, he took me to his rectory room and locked the door. It became clear he wanted something more than friendship. I sought a transfer to another school, but he continued to be in touch. After his proposal of marriage during my first year in the new position, I began to entertain thoughts of leaving the convent. A short time later, he received permission for further study and changed his proposal to a desire for a special relationship within the confines of the religious life style.

Soon after that experience, I was working as director of a retreat. I encountered more than friendly remarks from another priest who was doing the preaching at the retreat. That finalized my decision to leave the religious life. It was the week-end of my twenty-ninth birthday.

A Permanent Leave of Absence

My world came toppling down. I had worked hard for several years now to re-establish my self-esteem and to become truly pleasing to God, only to see clearly that I could no longer continue in this life style. I had seen first hand an hypocrisy that made my keeping of the vows ludicrous. I began the process of contacting the superiors and making the necessary arrangements for an obligatory leave of absence, although I knew I would never return to the religious life.

In the basement of the convent, I secretly wrote resumes and letters of introduction to public school superintendents. My family made it clear I was not expected to come home to live or to anticipate any help. A friend I had made while teaching in the new school offered to me a stay in her home while she and her husband and two small children were away on a business trip. The previous summer I had worked for a pharmaceutical firm as a research microbiologist and could return to that position at the end of the school year. A lay teacher was selling some very used furniture. The congregation I was leaving gave me two hundred dollars, which they were bound by canon law to return to me. Upon entering the group, I had been required to pay a fee which was considered as a form of dowry reminiscent of medieval times. I asked to stay in the convent until my board ran out at the end of August but was told Sister Nicoletta was waiting for my room. I was expected to be gone by the fifteenth. Fortunately, I was able to be hired just before the fifteenth of June for a position near my parents' home in a local public high school.

"Our wedding day"

I stayed in my friends' home while working the summer job and then moved into an apartment with my one hundred dollars' worth of used furniture. In the beginning of September, I began teaching in the public high school.

Six months later I signed my papers from Rome releasing me from my perpetual vows. I was told by the Superior it was only a piece of paper, but I had seen it as a life commitment to God. I had lost my chance to serve Him in the best way I knew possible. Now I was a lay person, defrocked of any possibility for total sanctification.

Marriage

Living alone in an apartment brought its own kind of loneliness. After eschewing the company of several other women, I missed the commitment of living with others on a daily basis. Getting married seemed to be the only answer, but most of my age group seemed to be married. The options had narrowed considerably during the years I had spent cloistered in the convent. I contacted a friend who had left two years before me. She suggested joining a dating service, as another former member of the congregation had recently met and married a fine gentleman in this manner. After a year of making contacts through such a service, I was introduced to Briant Doran. The moment our eyes met, a profound and enduring relationship began to unfold.

As we returned to my apartment on our first date, Briant shared how he had wanted to attend a boarding high school in preparation for becoming a priest. It was suggested to him by a friend that he wait until after high school. The interlude made it clear to Briant that a life of celibacy was not for him. I then shared my sixteen years of association with the Sisters of Charity of Saint Elizabeth. He had attended a high school staffed by the same Order and knew several of the nuns I had become acquainted with in my years of affiliation with them. In fact, we grew up unbeknown to each other in the same city in different parishes. He, too, had been raised by an Irish Catholic family and considered himself of the "fifties" generation. He had attended the installment of one of his cousins as Bishop over a diocese in Connecticut. Another cousin, John Doran, had become a priest in New Jersey and would marry us eighteen months later.

First Introduction to Truth

During the months of dating, Briant told me of Tom, who had left the Catholic Church. Briant, although a fallen-away Catholic at the time, tried to convince Tom to return to his Catholic faith. While working together, Tom took Briant to his church where Briant learned of a new and different way to look at the things of God. The pastor made it clear in the service he attended that *"all have sinned, and come short of the glory of God"* (Romans 3:23). *"There is none righteous, no not one"* (Romans 3:10), and *"all our righteousnesses are as filthy rags"* (Isaiah 64:6). Of ourselves we are permanently estranged from God. Only the blood of Jesus Christ shed on Calvary's cross can make us right with God, *"and with His stripes we are healed"* (Isaiah 53:5). *"For the wages of sin is death; but the gift of God is eternal life through Jesus Christ our Lord"* (Romans 6:23). The Bible was presented as the only source for faith and living.

Briant answered the invitation to trust Jesus by faith alone for his salvation. *"For by grace are ye saved through faith; and that not of yourselves; it is the gift of God; Not of works, lest any man should boast"* (Ephesians 2:8, 9). *"Behold, God is my salvation; I will trust and not be afraid; for the Lord Jehovah is my strength and my song; he also is become my salvation. Therefore with joy shall ye draw water out of the wells of salvation"* (Isaiah 12:2, 3).

Immediately he saw the need to make this message clear to those in the Catholic Church who were **trusting their works** to make them right with God. And the saddest part of the doing of the works was that one could never be sure when a person died whether he or she had done enough works to make it through the pearly gates. Thus through the system of Mass cards, which are left in great numbers for the grieving family at a funeral home, people waste their money buying those cards in hopes of praying their loved ones into heaven. *"And it is appointed unto men once to die, but after this the judgment"* (Hebrews 9:27). Salvation is to be secured through faith in the sacrifice of Jesus for one's sin before death. One's destiny is sealed at the drawing of the last breath.

It was clear to Briant that salvation was by faith alone through the merits of Christ alone. A perfect sacrifice had been offered for the atonement of sin once and for all. There is no more need of priests, for we have a High Priest Who is able to identify with us in our weakness and Who has passed through the heavenlies and sits at the right hand of the Father interceding for us. *"And every priest standeth daily ministering and offering oftentimes the same sacrifices, which can never take away sins; But this man, after He had offered one sacrifice for sins for ever, sat down on the right hand of God; From henceforth expecting* [waiting] *till his enemies be made a footstool. For by one offering he hath perfected forever them that are sanctified"* (Hebrews 10:11-14).

Briant matriculated for the then newly initiated program for married deacons in the Catholic Church. We had been married for a year and our first son was three months old at the time. For eighteen months Briant faithfully attended classes two nights a week at the diocesan offices. He became known for his "Protestant views" on the authority of the Scripture, Mary, purgatory, birth control and other areas of belief. For Briant, there was *"one God, and one mediator between God and men, the man Christ Jesus; Who gave himself a ransom for all"* (1 Timothy 2:5). The intercession of Mary and the saints and the absolution of the priest were rendered powerless by the study of God's Word. When he told the priest-director he intended as a deacon to tell people of the free grace available through the shed blood of Jesus by faith alone, he was laughed at and called a "Jesus freak". Briant knew there was no future for him in the program and decided to leave the Catholic Church.

Suppression of Truth

We both marveled at the obvious knowledge of the truth coupled with the deliberate denial of it by that church's hierarchy. Briant spoke of their responsibility for leading so many souls to hell by denying them access to the truth. Anyone who took a true biblical stand was ridiculed and silenced. There was no alternative but to leave a system entrenched in the lies of hundreds of years' duration. No one soul or even several souls would change the course of so large a body of members. John Wycliffe, John Hus, Martin Luther, John Calvin, and so many others had been able to do no more than lead those chosen by God away from the lies of the Catholic Church and into true biblical knowledge of salvation and all truth. Now it was Briant's turn to break with the entrenchment of false doctrines taught for so many centuries by Rome.

Briant's Conviction

Briant chose a Bible believing church close to our home. As a fallen away Catholic, he saw things quite clearly. Because of the depth of my personal commitment within the Catholic Church, it would take me longer to discern the truth of God's Word versus the diabolical system of Rome. Although I had long believed that the Catholic Church was wrong about some of its doctrines, I had learned to take its error in stride and believe that a church could have both error and truth. I had read Hans Kung's contribution, *Infallibility*, and had concluded that the Pope could not always be right when he spoke **ex cathedra.**

As I had read the Acts of the Apostles, I had become convinced that the church of the first century had the correct format and grieved that it could not be so today. We had been taught that the Protestant churches were mere corruptions of the Catholic Church, commonly referred to as the one true church founded on Saint Peter as quoted from the Gospel, *"That thou are Peter, and upon this rock I will build my church; and the gates of hell shall not prevail against it"* (Matthew 16:18). I was forced, I thought, to accept a much less than perfect church because the "ideal" had not existed since the first century A.D. How could this little group of Christians, with whom my husband now chose to associate and who in 1979 were meeting in a renovated chicken coop, approximate the ideal of the Scriptures?

Biblical Truth versus Catholic Doctrine

Through a Christian radio program I came in contact with a ministry devoted solely to those of the Catholic faith. I wrote Bart Brewer of Mission to Catholics International. Listening to his interview on the radio, I identified with the difficulties he had encountered in leaving the Catholic Church. He had gone through Bible college twice in his quest to be de-programmed from Catholic doctrine. Yes, that was I. He sent books and pamphlets which clearly explained the differences in Biblical belief and Catholic doctrine. I began to understand.

There was the doctrine of salvation by faith alone, of the necessary sole mediation of Jesus' life, death, and resurrection alone for salvation. And what an eye-opener when I read Paul saying in 1 Timothy 4:1-3 that those would come in later times demanding that people not marry and that they abstain from meat, *"Now the Spirit speaketh expressly, that in the latter times some shall depart from the faith, giving heed to seducing spirits, and doctrines of devils; Speaking lies in hypocrisy; having their conscience seared with a hot iron; Forbidding to marry, and commanding to abstain from meats, which God hath created to be received with thanksgiving of them which believe and know the truth."* That certainly described the teachings I had thought were from God because they were taught by what I had believed to be God's church.

Truth and lies cannot exist together. Either one believes the Word of God as the infallible rule of faith or one must accept the contradictions to Scripture taught by the Catholic Church and one day join the father of lies, Satan himself, in the lake of fire eternally damned and separated from the God Who has prepared a sure way of faith for us that leads to eternal glory with Him for all who will believe solely on the Word of God and not on the mere doctrines of men.

My Eyes are Opened

Finally, I was able to shed the multiple lies of Catholic teaching. The Bible would provide all that is needed for doctrine and practice. *"All scripture is given by inspiration of God, and is profitable for doctrine, for reproof, for correction, for instruction in righteousness"* (2 Timothy 3:16). I would trust the work of Jesus on Calvary's cross alone for my salvation and sanctification. I would recognize that works have been prepared for us to do. *"For we are His workmanship, created in Christ Jesus unto good works, which God hath before ordained that we should walk in them"* (Ephesians 2:10). It is

God who works in us to will and to do of His good pleasure. I must trust God by faith alone for my salvation by grace alone through the shed blood of Jesus alone.

Believers Baptism

After the birth of our second son, Briant and I were re-baptized together. He had waited patiently for me to "catch up" to him. Although we had both been baptized as infants, the Bible made it clear to us that baptism is a sign of faith in Jesus Christ and must be done after consciously making a faith commitment to Him. *"Then Peter said unto them, Repent, and be baptized every one of you in the name of Jesus Christ for the remission of sins, and ye shall receive the gift of the Holy Ghost"* (Acts 2:38).

Home Ministry

A short time later one of Briant's uncles died. He had loved him dearly but was quite convinced that Uncle Johnny probably had died without trusting Jesus alone for his salvation. He longed to stop working at his job and enter full time ministry but after much deliberation, he decided his calling was to his family and the raising of his sons. He reasoned that the ministry could have adverse effects on his marriage and the raising of his children. He decided against it but entertained the idea of one day opening a soup kitchen and "feeding the poor and giving them the Gospel".

Briant did see, as the steward of his home, to make extra rooms available for use by whosoever might be in need of a place to stay. The pastor gave him related materials to read in preparation for such a ministry and referred several in need of such assistance to us over a period of four years spanning the births of our second and third sons. We ministered to a young deaf widow with a two-year-old son, a legally blind woman, a Cambodian refugee orphan, and a family who had lost their home through under-employment and foreclosure, among many others.

Full-Time Mom

We had also become convicted of the necessity of a full-time "Mommy" in the home for the raising of the children. I had dutifully resigned from my tenured position in the public school. "If Jesus is Lord of your life, He is Lord of when you have your children," Briant explained. We would let God decide when He would choose to fill the quiver, *"but the just live by His faith"* (Habakkuk 2:4).

Our first two boys attended a Christian school until "Daddy's" unemployment made it no longer feasible. We had also become aware that both boys had learning difficulties. The best solution seemed to be to homeschool the boys. A wonderful experience of lessons and field trips and association with other families began to unfold.

After fifteen years of employment with an air freight company as a manager, Briant was "let go" from the company after months of over-time to try to secure his position. We learned two years later of the buy-out of the company by another air freight company. It was clearly an economic measure to salvage a company in financial distress.

Briant remained steadfast in his position that I remain a full-time "Mommy". His conviction found expression in the words, "The Mommy is the heart of the home. Satan is breaking up the family. God will provide through me." There ensued seven and a half years of relative unemployment. Never was he able to work at a job for more than eight months' duration. He saw this time as a testing from God of his faith. During the second year of re-locating his position as provider, our fourth son, Austin, was born. It was the only time we had health insurance during the long stretch of seeking permanent employ-

"With my four sons"

ment. A caesarian section and the five day stay in the hospital were covered by the insurance. God showed Himself faithful in our commitment to let Him decide the timing of the births of our children. I continued to homeschool the boys.

Financial Collapse

Briant changed careers to insurance sales which he had had brief experience with during his single years. We refinanced our home at three strategic points to fill gaps in income between jobs. Several friends and relatives helped with our needs from time to time.

Eventually, it became necessary to file a Chapter Thirteen bankruptcy. Briant firmly believed that we were to stay in our home. We had used it for the glory of God during the years of providing hospitality for those in need. He said God doesn't give talents and then take them away. He multiplies them. We had used our first home for the Lord. He stood firm that we would not lose it. Psalm Thirty became his favorite prayer to the Lord, *"when I go down to the pit? Shall the dust praise thee"* (verse 9). He was convinced that God would see us through.

Briant's Witness Goes On

As Briant worked at what had become a third job on the Friday night before the first week in October, he experienced a heart attack and went quite suddenly to be with the Lord he had served so faithfully. His friend, Tom, who had led him to the Lord seventeen years before, had become a pastor of a church. He was willing to preach Briant's funeral and to give a stirring eulogy. "When Briant came to know the Lord, he never cooled down. He was always on fire for the Lord." Friends from the job he had lost seven and a half years before came many miles to say good-bye to Briant. One of them shared, "I never saw such faith in a man. He just kept going."

On his grave stone I would place the Scripture, "The dead in Christ shall rise first...even so Lord Jesus, come!" He hasn't cooled down yet. There he remains witnessing in the graveyard.

The Lord's Provision

Meanwhile, a call was placed to the lawyer's office to cancel the meeting to re-file the Chapter Thirteen bankruptcy. Briant's wake took precedence for that date. The notice of the foreclosure process came days after the funeral. I dutifully forwarded it to the lawyer. I had approximately $150,000 of debt and $90,000 from two insurance policies.

During this tumultuous experience, I looked back to the convent transition. If God could get me through all of that pain and confusion, He could get me through this crisis. Family had come to the funeral merely to satisfy their social obligations. Communications had ceased years before as we had become unacceptable in

150

our new-found biblical faith. My refusing to work outside our home while Briant was unemployed for seven and a half years had only strained relations further. Our help would truly come from the Lord, Who made heaven and earth. I remained convinced that God did not want me to return to work outside our home at this juncture. I would wait on Him to clearly show me His will.

After months of negotiating and processing, the lawyer for the bankruptcy was able to reduce the $125,000 in mortgages to a sale price of $82,000. Since there was only $90,000 of insurance it became clear that Briant's death had provided for the bumpy and yet steady functioning of the home to this day. The company he was working for when he died paid for the funeral expenses as part of the worker's compensation laws and sent a gift of $10,000 one month after his death. I continued delivering newspapers as I had done for the two years prior to his death. It had been the shifting of child to adult paper route. I had taken it on for my son that he could continue his entrepreneurial experience. Never did I dream that it would provide both before and after Briant's death for our survival.

Since Briant died working, I was able to obtain worker's compensation benefits which, along with Social Security payments and a very small pension from the company that let him go after fifteen years, provided for me to continue homeschooling and even to drop the paper route.

The deep ache in my heart when I left the convent and what I thought was the only and best way of serving God has turned into a joyous song of praise to God for the mighty works He has done in the places He has led me since. I have been the recipient of much grace over the years to the faithful performance of so many diversified experiences. The roles of wife and mother, teacher of academics for homeschooled children, of Bible studies for women, of Sunday school for children, founder and coordinator of a home-school support group and short-term teacher in two Christian schools has more than compensated for my "loss". And to do all of these "works" trusting the grace and sufficiency of Jesus' blood for my salvation and sanctification has simplified my experience tremendously.

No Turning Back

The road is narrow and few there are who find it, to paraphrase Matthew 7:13, 14. We must enter by the strait gate and look unto

Jesus alone, the Author and Perfecter of our faith. We must be daily in His Word, for *"faith cometh by hearing, and hearing by the word of God"* (Romans 10:17). We must launch out into the deep, trusting God for everything, for the just shall live by faith. His mercies—*"they are new every morning; great is Thy faithfulness"* (Lamentations 3:23). And *"Being confident of this very thing, that He which hath begun a good work in you will perform it until the day of Jesus Christ"* (Phillipians 1:6). *"For it is God who works in me to will and to do of His good pleasure* (Phillipians 2:13).

At one juncture my husband shared an interesting paraphrase of Scripture when he said, "I'm walking on the water and I'm out so far I can't turn back." His conviction to maintain his home as God would have it despite great hardship has brought untold blessing, both material and spiritual, to his family. We will forever revel in that blessing.

Trust and Obey

My oldest son is now engaged to a born-again believer. They are both nineteen years old. Briant, Jr. is attending a computer school where he maintains his position on the Dean's List. He works full-time for an ambulance service as a certified EMT. Together this young couple is planning to pursue the values we have taught. "Mommy" will stay home and raise the children. Jesus will be the Lord of conception. My son has stated emphatically that there can be no fear of hard times. He knows faith is the answer to God's provision. "God is still getting His remnant ready," as his Dad used to say. We have but, as the hymn so rightly says, to "trust and obey, for there's no other way to be happy in Jesus but to trust and obey".

There are times when I think in comparative terms with Joseph's life in Genesis. There are so many pieces of the puzzle that would seem to be extraneous to the sense of my life. But *"I know whom I have believed and am persuaded that He is able to keep that which I've committed unto Him against that day"* (2 Timothy 1:12). He has numbered every hair on my head and ordained each of my days before one of them ever existed. From eternity, my life has been mapped out. Great is His faithfulness. His ways are not our ways, but His ways are perfect. I need only trust in Him with all my heart and lean not on my own understanding. He is creating His tapestry. I see the knots and criss-crosses on the back side. He sees the finished and perfected work on the "right" side.

He has saved me from my sin by faith alone in His Son, Jesus. He has delivered me out of the diabolical system of works that is the Catholic Church and has shown me that all is of grace. All of eternity will not be long enough to thank and praise Him for His wonderful deeds to the children of men. To God be the glory! Great things He has done and continues to do!

Wilma Sullivan

(formerly Sister Wilma Marie, R.S.M.)

Ex-Nun Finds Peace with God

My Desire To Do Good

"Sincere" and "zealous" are the words that describe the religious aspects of my life for twenty-nine and a half years as a Roman Catholic. I so desired to do what was right. I went to Mass, received the sacraments, loved my neighbors, and basically tried to do good to all people, and I always thought that this was the way to get to heaven. The desire to do good to all people led me to become a member of a religious order, the Sisters of Mercy, from 1967 to 1971.

My Search For Truth

My quest for truth began at an altar rail approximately six months before I actually left the convent in March of 1971. I was kneeling at communion time, and the priest held the host before my face and said, "The body of Christ." Before I could respond with my automatic and expected reply of "Amen", a question entered my mind for the first time—"Is it really?" Of course, I had no time to analyze that thought before my response, but **daily** thereafter that same question was there in my thoughts—"Is it really?" Finally, I began to pray with sincerity, "God, if Jesus is in this host, show me He is; but if He's not, show me the truth."

"I become a member of the Sisters of Mercy"

155

Within six months of that prayer, I was out of the convent, and before the end of two and a half years I had been led to the truth of God's Word about this very question. On November 11, 1973, I came to the place in my life where I realized that I needed to trust in the all-sufficient sacrifice of Christ and in the blood He shed for the forgiveness of my sins, and I become a born-again child of God **by faith alone!**

Good Works Are Not Enough

The Lord used a medical problem in my life to put me in the place of sweet confrontation with a born-again Christian lady in Pennsylvania to help me to see my desperately lost spiritual condition before Him. I entered the hospital for minor surgery in October of 1973. Although I was only there a short time and did not know this lady well, I kept in contact with her daily for the next week about her physical condition. She invited me to her home to talk about spiritual things, and since she knew I was an ex-nun and with my feeling that she needed someone to talk with, I accepted her invitation. Two of her friends were there at her home, and for the first time in my life my religion was challenged. The most important thing I learned from this talk was that all the good works a person could do during his lifetime are not what makes it possible for him to go to heaven. Isaiah 64:6 states, "*All our righteousnesses are as filthy rags*," and again in Ephesians 2:8-9 it is stated, "*For by grace are ye saved, through faith; and that not of yourselves; it is the gift of God, not of works, lest any man should boast.*" Therefore, what saves him from going to hell is not his good works, but his faith alone in Jesus Christ as his personal Savior.

During our discussion that first night I was invited to go to their church, Calvary Baptist Church in Lansdale, Pennsylvania. I did go, and after the second Sunday of going to Mass at the Catholic Church and then going to their church, I asked to speak to their pastor, Dr. E. Robert Jordan, just to talk about my life and where I was headed. While he was speaking with me, he gave me his testimony of how he was saved and what the Lord had done for him. He made a statement to me that made me stop dead in my tracks. He said, "Wilma, I never knew that I was bad enough to go to hell just by being born into this world, and nothing takes away the penalty of sin but the blood of Jesus Christ." At that moment the Holy Spirit helped me to understand my lost condition and that I needed to be saved. Ever since I was a child, I had been taught that God was a loving God and it would take a pretty bad person to go to hell, and that if I would try to be good, go to confession when I was bad, and receive communion as often as possible, I would go to heaven if I died without any sins on my soul. I came to realize that I was a sinner purely by being born into this world and that no baptism could take away that sin because "without the shedding of blood there is no remission [of sin]," and that I needed to accept Him as **my** personal Saviour.

Can I Remain a Catholic?

As soon as I accepted Christ as my personal Saviour, many questions began to well up within my soul. The Lord had already provided the lady from the hospital who was willing and able to answer these questions for me from the Word of God. One of the first questions I asked her was, "Can I be saved and remain a Catholic?" Her response was a very wise one: "Wilma, I don't believe you can, but I'm not going to tell you that you can't. I will just show you what the Bible says about worshipping God. You tell me how you are worshipping Him now, and we will see if they agree. Then you decide for yourself what to do."

A verse of Scripture was given to me on which to base all of my decisions, John 4:24: "*God is a Spirit; and they that worship Him* **must** *worship Him in* **spirit** *and* **truth**." I was so sincerely searching for the truth, and I loved God so much, I wanted to make sure that He was hearing my worship. I knew that God would not and could not lie to me, but on the other hand, I knew that man could and does make mistakes. I became like the Bereans of Acts 17:11, searching the Scriptures daily to see whether or not the things these people were telling me were true.

As I compared the sacraments of Catholicism—communion, baptism, penance, etc.—with the Bible, I discovered problems. I asked the lady who was helping me about communion, and she was able to answer my ever-present question, "Is it really?" She said, "Of course, Jesus doesn't need to die at every Mass." She showed me that Christ died "*once for all*" (Hebrews 10:10-14) on Calvary's cruel cross and uttered His "*It is finished*" (John 19:30) to seal that fact. Needless to say, I was thrilled that my question was finally answered.

I continued my examination of the sacraments with anxiety, and yet I was confident that I would find the truth of how I must be worshipping God. With regard to "baptism", the Bible, I found, declares that it is only an outward expression of the inward repentance that has taken place in a sinner (Acts 2:41; 8:26-39; 16:25-34), while Catholicism claims that the rite of baptism takes away original sin and makes a person a child of God. I also discovered that in the sacrament of penance the priest has the power to forgive a person for his sins; however, this is unscriptural because the Bible states that there is only **one** God and **one** mediator between God and men, the man Christ Jesus (1 Timothy 2:5) and **no one else**! I also came to realize that there is no act of penance (either in the form of prayers or of good works) that can pay for my sins. Only Christ's *"once for all"* sacrifice could do that.

A Difficult Decision

These obvious contradictions with Scripture (and many others) confronted me with the most important and difficult decision I had ever had to make, to **believe** God Who cannot lie (Romans 3:4) and follow His way in the Bible or **believe man** who can make mistakes (Proverbs 14:12). On December 16, 1973, I decided to

leave Catholicism, do only what the Bible commanded, and simply leave the results with God. To this day, I can honestly testify that I have never regretted my decision and have, by His love which constrains me, *"(grown) in the grace and knowledge of (my) Lord and Saviour Jesus Christ"* (2 Peter 3:18).

"I can testify to God's faithfulness"

Truth Sets Free

I extend a personal invitation to you who read this testimony to ask the Lord to show you the truth and let that truth set you free from mere church tradition. Trust Christ as your all-sufficient Saviour and Lord. He will give you a **precious** relationship with Him and not just a religion. I pray that you will believe and receive Him and His truth today.

Peggy O'Neill
(formerly Sister Aidan, RSHM)

I Had Never Heard the True Gospel

"But to him that worketh not, but believeth on Him that justifieth the ungodly, his faith is counted for righteousness." Romans 4:5

I served as a sister in a religious order for about fifty years and during all that time, I had never heard the true Gospel. Certain things may be let ride, but when it comes to the Gospel there can be no compromise because the Gospel is the power of God for salvation. A false gospel cannot have that power and any church that preaches a perverted gospel is depriving its members of the foundational and most essential message, the message of salvation.

False Teachers in the Early Church

In the Bible we read of the churches in Galatia where false teachers were leading people into another gospel. They were going back under law, for as well as believing in Jesus Christ, they had to observe certain religious laws making Christianity a set of rules and laws whereby they had to earn heaven. Galatians Chapter Three tells us that Christ has redeemed us from the curse of the law and that He is the end of the law for righteousness. If we take Jesus plus any religious law as a means of salvation we are fallen from grace. We cannot trust in law and grace at the same

"I was a nun for fifty years."

time, so trying to combine the two, we put ourselves under law. By adding anything to the finished work of the cross, Christ will profit us nothing. Galatians 3:21 says that if righteousness comes by the law then Christ died in vain. This is the seriousness of being under the law—we have to be our own saviors and the Bible says that no man can be saved by keeping the law. It is not surprising, therefore, that the Apostle Paul in his Epistle to the Galatians used strong words to say that if anyone, even an angel from heaven were to preach another gospel, let him be accursed.

My Attempts to Live by the Law

Like the Galatians, I was trying to save myself by a combination of law and grace. I was putting my faith in Jesus but also in my own actions, trying to earn heaven and the things of God by doing the best I could instead of receiving salvation as a gift. The Gospel was no longer Good News, for the burden of salvation was on my back. In the end, I could only **hope** to be saved in spite of all my attendance at Mass, the sacraments, prayers, and other good works. By offering my own righteousness as a means of being accepted before God, I was, according to Galatians 5:3, making myself a debtor to the whole law. I was obligated to meet a standard of perfection that equals that of God. I had never understood how to trust Jesus and Him alone as my Savior. I had not known that it was not by my performance, but by just believing and accepting the perfect price Jesus paid when He shed His blood for me on Calvary that I would be saved. When I heard the true message of the Gospel, the truth set me free. I praise God that I am learning to depend more and more on the Lord Jesus for my needs, both in this life and for eternity.

Famine in Ireland

A catechism of the Catholic Church gives this teaching, "The Bishops have the mission of preaching the Gospel to every creature so that all may attain salvation through faith, Baptism and the observance of the Commandments." This preaches a gospel of works. By mixing law and grace, the Catholic Church has fallen into the same error as the Galatians. A church that acknowledges much of the truth of the Word of God but that misrepresents the Gospel is the kind of church into which I was born in Ireland. I was told it was the one true Church and for over sixty years, I never once doubted or questioned that.

The second of ten children, I had the example of good parents who were faithful members of their Church. Were my family to be judged by the teachings and traditions of the Catholic Church, we could all reasonably hope for a place in heaven. But the Bible tells us that we will be judged, not by the teachings of any Church, but by the Word of God. *"The Word that I have spoken, the same shall judge him in the last day"* (John 12:48). In my young days, there was not a single copy of the Bible in our home. Happily, today things in that regard have changed.

Here in Ireland, we still talk about the Great Famine of the 1840's when the potato crop failed and a million people died of starvation, while another million emigrated to America never again to return home. Ireland in the 1990's is a land of abundance, but there is a famine of a different kind, a famine described in the Bible, *"Behold the days come, saith the Lord God, That I will send a famine in the land, not a famine of bread, nor a thirst for water, But of hearing the Words of the Lord"* (Amos 8:11). Those days of famine have surely come to Ireland, yet it is encouraging to know that more and more people have been meeting together for some years to study the Bible and feast upon the Word of the Lord.

My Mother's Death in Ireland

In England where I spent most of my religious life, I was an enthusiastic believer in the Charismatic Movement, considered to have been a genuine move of the Holy Spirit. I also attended some Christian meetings with thousands of Christians from many nations. When I got permission from my religious superiors to come home to care for my mother in the last six years of her life, I had the opportunity to listen to Christian radio programs where the Gospel of salvation was regularly preached. When my mother died, aged ninety-five, I did not have an understanding of the Gospel so I was unable to help her have an assurance of her salvation. However, I recall with joy her words to me on the day she died, "I want Jesus to come for me today." These were precious words. Also during those years at home, I had contact with a nephew of mine, Tom Griffin, who had a godly influence on my life. He had joined a Christian church and he introduced me to J.P. Walsh who was the leader of a local group in weekly Bible study. All this eventually led up to my discovering the unconditional love of God and the liberating message of the Gospel.

Christ's Righteousness Available to Me

"Righteousness" was the key word that opened for me the truth of the Gospel. I found the word in Paul's description of the Gospel in Romans 1:16. The Gospel "...*is the power of God unto salvation to everyone that believeth;...for in it is the righteousness of God revealed.*" The righteousness of God—this is what is required to get to heaven. What God demands is perfection: *nothing less than His own righteousness.* This was something new to me for all I was ever conscious of was *my own righteousness* and how I could save my soul. I could have been compared to those Jews in Romans 10:3, "*For they, being ignorant of God's righteousness, and going about to establish their own righteousness, have not submitted themselves to the righteousness of God.*" I was ignorant of God's righteousness. What it takes for salvation is a righteousness that equals that of God and I knew that no one could ever reach that standard. This then is what the Gospel is all about: what God demands, He provides. The Good News is that if we believe in Jesus Christ whose death on the cross, burial and resurrection has paid the price of our sin, we will be saved. The Bible puts it this way, "*Jesus who knew no sin became sin for us that we might be made the righteousness of God in Him*" (2 Corinthians 5:21). In exchange for my sins, God will give me the righteousness of Jesus, God's righteousness for my sins! This is the Good News, the Gospel in a nutshell.

Salvation by Grace

God's Word tells us that salvation is by grace alone. I soon found out why salvation is a **gift** from God and cannot be by **works**. Isaiah 64:6 says, "*All our righteousnesses are as filthy rags*" when compared with the infinite righteousness of God. All my best efforts, my faithfulness, my good works are nothing but filthy rags when it comes to earning heaven. I could never earn heaven, so Jesus did it for me. I just come to God empty handed, not with all my "great" keeping of laws, my penance and my holiness. My dependence is totally on Jesus and what He has done for me. Paul, once a religious Jew who had strictly adhered to the law, came to the place where he said he wanted to know nothing but Christ and Him crucified. We, too, must come to that place of dependency, not on ourselves, not on Mary or any church—all our dependency must be on Christ. We look to Him and Him alone. Even though our good lives will never gain heaven for us, there is a purpose in living an upright life in our day-to-day relationships with our families and others. This, too, is provided for by God's grace in the direction of His Word and the power of His Spirit given to us the moment we believe. Salvation is on the basis of our faith in Jesus Christ, not on the basis of our conduct. That same faith keeps us trusting in Jesus Christ as we walk daily by His Spirit.

I had never heard the full story of Redemption, how completely Jesus had dealt with sin to save us from hell, *"the lake of fire and brimstone, where the beast and the false prophet are, and shall be tormented day and night forever and ever"* (Revelation 20:10). Jesus did not partially deal with sin. He did such a complete and finished work that all sin was blotted out and washed away by His precious blood. Sin, past, present and future, even those sins not yet committed were forgiven two thousand years ago when Jesus died on that cross on Calvary. God does not keep a record of the believer's sins. *"I, even I, am he who blotteth out thy transgressions for mine own sake, and I will not remember thy sins"* (Isaiah 43:25). The debt of sin has been completely paid, yet not everyone will be saved. There is one thing that will send people to hell. Jesus Himself spoke about it in John 16:9, *"they believe not on Me"*, a rejection of Jesus and the salvation He gained for us. God does not violate the will of any person, nor is salvation automatic. Man is born condemned, separated from God as a son of Adam, but God's will is for all men to be saved and to come to a knowledge of the truth. For those who believe in Christ, *"There is therefore now no comdemnation to them which are in Christ Jesus"* (Romans 8:1).

God's Justice Satisfied

"The jury is still out" is what a priest recently said in this context. According to Romans Chapter Three, the jury has already pronounced the verdict, "Guilty". *"There is none righteous, no, not one."* The religious and the unreligious are all guilty before God. In His justice, God had to impose a penalty for sin, and since man could never pay that penalty, God in His love found a way to do for us what we ourselves could not do. He gave His Son, Jesus, who took all the blame for us and in our place He was condemned to death. He died on the cross. Jesus was forsaken by His Father. He descended into hell and took from Satan the keys of hell and death. The heavenly courts of eternal justice were satisfied and the believer's debt was fully paid. On the third day Jesus was raised from the dead by the Holy Spirit, Jesus the first born-from the dead, the first born of many brethren. Man must accept Jesus' sacrifice to be saved and when he does, God accepts him on the basis of His Son's righteousness.

Relationship with God Restored in Christ

As time went on, I saw that in the Scriptures our relationship with God is based on both God's **grace** and **faith**. His plan for our salvation is that we should believe in Christ Jesus by grace through faith. *"For by grace are ye saved through faith; and that not of ourselves, it is the gift of God"* (Ephesians 2:8). Faith is not a gift we get from our parents or from the church, *"Faith cometh by hearing, and hearing by the Word of God"* (Rom 10:17). In God's plan for salvation, faith itself, by which we trust only on Christ and His completed work, is of itself the work of God. This was the message Jesus gave the people in John 6:28-29 when they asked what they should do that they might work the works of God. Jesus said to them, *"This is the work of God, that ye believe on Him whom he [God] has sent"*. I would have said that I had always believed in Jesus, yet now I realize that I had not known the real Jesus, the Jesus revealed in the Scriptures. I had known nothing of the gift of righteousness He had to offer or of the complete forgiveness of sin brought about by His death and resurrection. Titus 1:16 says, *"They profess that they know God, but in works they deny Him...."* I was carrying out religious practices that showed that I did not know Him. I thought it was essential for my salvation to attend Mass because I had not fully accepted His propitiatory sacrifice on the cross. I sought forgiveness for sin in the Sacrament of Reconciliation, not knowing that Jesus had already reconciled me to God. As well as depending on Jesus, I also depended on Mary, the saints, my penances and good works, my hours of adoration before the Blessed Sacrament, rosaries, scapulars, indulgences, purgatory. Paul uses a word to describe the value of anything we try to do to add to the work of Jesus, it is the word *"dung"* (Philippians 3:8). All our good works are displeasing to God if offered as a means of gaining heaven for ourselves or for others, implying that what Jesus did on Calvary was not enough.

Repentance from Dead Works

According to Hebrews 6:1, one of the foundations of the Christian life is repentance or turning away from dead works. By dead works is meant religious practices and good works performed either by oneself or through the ministry of the church so as to obtain salvation. All these works, no matter how righteous, are the filthy rags referred to in Isaiah 64:6. They are what is called religion and religion is man's counterfeit for Jesus Christ. There is no promise in the Bible that says religious people will go to heaven. On the contrary, Jesus called the most religious people on earth in His time, the Pharisees, to repentance. The Bible tells us that to be declared righteous before God, the first thing we must do is stop working for it. This was very strange to me, who as a Catholic had been led to put so much emphasis on my own performance as well as on the ministry of priests. Once heard, the Word of God must take first place and God's Word in Romans 4:5 left me in no doubt, *"But to him that **worketh not** but **believeth** on Him that justifieth the ungodly, his **faith** is counted for righteousness."*

I had never really believed, as I had never accepted salvation as a gift. By God's mercy, I was convicted of the sin of not totally trusting in Jesus and His finished work. I repented from dead works and from trusting in my own righteousness and I accepted the finished work of Jesus on the cross. I had now really heard the Word of salvation and with the Word came God's gift of supernatural faith. As in 2 Corinthians Chapter Four, I believed therefore I spoke and committed my life to Jesus Christ trusting in Him as my Savior. At that instant, God imparted to me His righteousness. In my new born-again spirit, I was as righteous as God, not because of any goodness of mine but because of Jesus. What had happened to me is described in 2 Corinthians 5:17. I experienced salvation. I was born again in the way that Jesus said to Nicodemus, *"you must be born again"*. I was baptized into Christ. For the first time I knew that my name was written in the Lamb's Book of Life.

Baptism into Jesus Christ

What had happened to me is what the Bible calls **baptism into Jesus Christ**. Romans 6:3, *"As many of us as were **baptized into Jesus Christ** were baptized into His death"*. Galatians 3:27, *"for as many of you as have been **baptized into Christ** have put on Christ."* There was no external ceremony, no priest, no godparents. It was a matter

"After my baptism on Banna Strand"

between God the Father, Son and Holy Spirit, and me. I had been immersed spiritually into Christ.

A short time afterwards, I was baptized by immersion in the Atlantic Ocean at a place called Banna Strand in my native County Kerry. This baptism in water by immersion is an expression of the inner change that had already taken place in my spirit. It was a public confession of my belief in Jesus Christ as Savior and a showing forth of His death, burial and resurrection. Baptism in water does not make a person a Christian, it shows that he already is a Christian. The Catholic Church has lost this truth of the baptism into Jesus Christ, the baptism that translates us from the kingdom of Satan into the kingdom of God. For this reason it can be said that many are Christian only in name.

Catholic Infant Baptism

Paul in reference to the baptism into Jesus, speaks in Colossians 2:11 of the circumcision of the heart, a circumcision made **without hands**. I was one day old when I was taken to the local Catholic Church to be baptized. The hands of the priest signed me with the sign of the cross, anointed me with oil and chrism and put salt on my lips. There was a laying on of hands and hands were used to pour water on my head. My baptism, outwardly a beautiful and symbolic ceremony, was in reality nothing but an empty ritual. Baptism in water is a biblical ordinance that Christians obey after believing in Jesus. In the Acts of the Apostles 10:44-47, there is an example of Christian baptism for New Testament believers. In verse 47, baptism in water is given only **after** Cornelius and his household were saved and filled with the Holy Spirit. In Ireland there was an incident recently where a baby died, days before it was to be baptized. That the baby died without baptism added to the parents' grief. The Catholic Church in her liturgy could only invite them to trust in the mercy of God and pray for their child's salvation. However, according to the Word of God, that child went straight to heaven. It is true that everyone is born in original sin (in Adam), but Romans 5:13 tells that *"sin is not imputed where there is no law."* The law does not apply until a child comes to the use of reason or the age of discernment. Paul wrote, *"For I was alive apart from the law once; but when the commandment came, sin revived, and I died"* (Romans 7:9). The false doctrines relating to baptism are a betrayal of the trust of millions of sincere Catholics who are misled as to their true standing before

God in an area where their quality of life here on earth and their eternity is at stake. Until about eight years ago, I would have strongly opposed anything said against the Catholic Church, and even as I set about writing this testimony, my intention was to avoid any adverse criticism. But things have not worked out that way and any criticism of mine is only of the system into which I was born.

Understanding the Bible

Some people say that the Bible is hard to understand and this is true if one fails to grasp certain foundational truths. One of those truths is the concept that man is a **spirit** being with a **soul** (mind, will, and emotions) and he lives in a **body**. In I Thessalonians 5:23 we see how God divides man, *"spirit, soul and body"* and Hebrews 4:12 talks about the Word of God *"piercing even to the dividing asunder of the soul and spirit."* Catholic doctrine attributes to the soul what the Bible attributes to the spirit making no distinction between the two. Without a knowledge of this distinction, there was much in the Bible that I could not understand. I could not understand Scripture truths like the righteousness of the believer or "as He is, so are we in this world". To live the Christian life it is important to know how our spirit, soul and body function and relate to one another so that by the power of the Holy Spirit, the recreated spirit may dominate the body and soul which will not be free from the presence of sin until the believer experiences physical death.

Some time ago, a story was told in our church of a poor man who owned one field. He had barely enough to live on, but had he known, he could have been a wealthy man, for underneath that field was an oil well. This man's story is that of many of us Christians today. Inside us is a spiritual "oil well", and we are not aware of the limitless resources of God within us. It is possible that the early Christians knew and lived by the power of the Holy Spirit that was available in their born-again spirits. With the true Gospel message, they turned the then known world upside down in the first twenty to thirty years of Christianity. In our born-again spirits, God has provided everything we need and His life will be manifested through our lives to the degree that we renew our minds with His Word and use the grace He makes available moment by moment. The Bible tells us in I Corinthians 1:30 that Jesus *"...is made unto us wisdom, and righteousness, and sanctification, and redemption."*

My Religious Order

At seventeen, I left home to enter the Order of the Religious of the Sacred Heart of Mary. This is an International Order founded by Fr. Jean Pierre Gailhac at Beziers in the south of France. I spent the first seven years of my religious life in France and then after training as a teacher in England, I devoted thirty-five years to teaching in parish schools governed by the Local Education Authority. Side by side with life as a teacher was my religious life considered by me to be the highest calling. During all my years in the convent, I never had any reason to think otherwise. After the period of six years at home caring for my mother, I would have returned to the convent to work and share with the nuns I respected, loved and knew so well. A younger sister of mine, Carmel, is a member of the order and she is presently teaching African children in Zambia. However, it was not possible for me to return to the convent as I no longer could agree with the teachings and practices of the Catholic Church. Soon, I no longer viewed the religious life as being the highest calling. Richard Bennett, once a Dominican priest, writing in an article, "Is the Religious Form of Life Designed by God?", says that the Bible has ordained only three different institutions: the family, the church and the state. Religious life could not be reconciled with the Word of God.

Freed from the Law

Having been under law for so much of my life, the Epistle to the Galatians is of particular interest to me. In addition to being subject to the Ten Commandments and other church laws, religious life has its own rules, constitutions and vows. The Bible, however, speaks of only one law for New Testament believers, not the law of works, but the law of Jesus Christ, a law written on our hearts. Jesus Himself is the reality of the Mosaic Law which like everything else in the Old Covenant was only a type and shadow of things to come. "The Commandments of Ordinances were nailed to the cross", and the part that remained was the spirit and intent of the law—that we love God with all our hearts and our neighbors as ourselves. This law is the very nature of Jesus Himself living today through an individual in the flesh. He is not looking at our outward observances. He wants to find people who yield themselves to Him so completely that He can live His nature in them from the inside out. We have a description of the nature and character of Jesus in Galatians 5:22-23, "*the fruit of the Spirit is love, joy,* peace, long-suffering, gentleness, goodness, faith, meekness, self-control." On earth Jesus was a living manifestation of the fruit of the Spirit. This is not a list of pleasant qualities that improve our personalities, but the character of Jesus Christ. In our lives it is manifested when by grace through faith we allow His Spirit rather than our sinful natures to be in control. Romans 8:29 says that God has predestined believers to be conformed to the image of His Son. In our lives there can be joy instead of discouragement, peace rather than confusion and strife, the loving, wholesome word instead of the impatient or unkind word.

Instead of subjecting ourselves to the law of Moses, we let Christ live His life in us through His Spirit who enables us in our weakness. This is the law Jesus referred to in Matthew Chapter Five, *"that whoever shall do it and teach by example shall be called great in the kingdom of heaven."* Religious life with its rules and vows is not God's way as defined in the Scriptures. Religious vows of poverty, chastity and obedience are not found in Scripture. Jesus directs us in Matthew 5:34-37, *"..Swear not at all, neither by heaven, for it is God's throne, nor by the earth, for it is his footstool...neither shalt thou swear by thy head...but let your communication be 'Yea, yea; Nay, nay; for whatever is more than these cometh of evil."* What is spoken of in the New Testament is the **priesthood of all believers.** Peter writes that every true believer is a member of a *"royal priesthood"* (1 Peter 2:9). Jesus is our High Priest and believers in Christ are priests with a divine call and purpose to offer up spiritual sacrifices, the sacrifice of a yielded heart, offering praise to God in all things and invited to a ministry of intercession on behalf of others.

One Mediator, Jesus Christ

The Epistle to the Hebrews was written to bring people from the Old Covenant way of serving God into the New Covenant realities that Jesus Christ brought into effect. Sad to say, the transition has not yet been made two thousand years later. The Catholic Church still has the law and the priesthood. In her liturgy there is the sacrifice and the altar, priestly vestments, incense, candles, all of which were essential to Jewish religion and worship. These were Old Testament types and shadows of things to come. The Catholic Church has christianized Judaism and not come into the New Covenant established by the finished work of Jesus on the cross. For years, at Mass I heard the words, "This is the blood of the New and Everlasting Covenant." I knew little or nothing about that Covenant. I was operating under an Old Covenant mentality. The Catholic Church ordains priests to perpetrate the Sacrifice of the Cross, claiming that God still needs to be appeased for sin. To quote from a Catholic catechism, "Each sacrifice of the Mass appeases God's **wrath** against sin." Contrary to this, God says in His Word, "*So have I sworn that I would not be **wrath** with you or rebuke you.*" And in Hebrews 8:12, "*I will be merciful to their unrighteousness, and their sins and their iniquities I will remember no more.*"

A priesthood and sacrifice of atonement to cover for a broken law were imperative under the Mosaic Law, but in New Testament times, there is no priesthood (apart from the priesthood of believers) and no sacrifice (apart from the finished offering of Jesus Christ who paid the sin debt in full). We no longer need priests to stand before God as mediators, nor has any believer more direct access to God than another. We are all invited to come boldly to the throne of grace, to come to our Father, standing in the righteousness of His Son which is imputed to all who believe in Him. We can directly worship, find mercy and help in every need. Like so many men and women in religious orders, priests are men whose desire is to love and serve God, but the Roman Catholic priesthood dishonors Jesus Christ and His once-for-all sacrifice on Calvary. Their role as mediators usurps the present-day ministry in heaven of Jesus Christ, our only Mediator, Advocate and High Priest.

Mariolatry

The same can be said of the place given to Mary, the mother of Jesus. She is given titles that rightly belong to God, even the Father, Son and Holy Spirit. She is called Mother of Mercy, the All Holy, Mother of the Living, Seat of Wisdom, Gate of Heaven, Advocate, Mediatrix, Co-Redeemer, the litany goes on and on. Pope Benedict XIII wrote, "The Blood shed for us and those members which He offered to the Father, the wounds He received as the price of our liberty are no other than the flesh and blood of Mary. Thus she with Christ redeemed mankind." Medical science, however, confirms that a child gets its blood from the father. Therefore, the blood of Jesus was the blood of God (Acts 20:28), the precious blood of the Everlasting Covenant. We were redeemed with "*the precious blood of Christ, as of a lamb without blemish and without spot*" (1 Peter 1:19). Pope Paul VI in "The Credo of the People of God" gave Mary her newest title, Mary, Mother of the Church. In John 19:27, the words of Jesus from the cross, *"Behold thy mother!"*, are interpreted as a declaration of Mary to be mother over the whole church. It is significant that in John's three epistles there is not even a mention of Mary's name, neither is there a reference to her in any of the other New Testament epistles which were written to the churches for guidance in matters of doctrine, worship, and church discipline. Had John interpreted the words of Jesus from the cross as the Catholic Church has done, he would surely have exhorted people to look upon Mary as their mother to whom they could entrust their cares and petitions.

There is no biblical evidence of anyone praying to Mary or giving her the *hyperdulia* type of veneration recommended by the Catholic Church. The present Pope, John Paul II, speaking of Mary's suffering said, "It was on Calvary that Mary's suffering beside the suffering of Jesus reached an intensity which can hardly be imagined from a human point of view, but which was mysteriously and supernaturally fruitful for the redemption of the world." It is not surprising that a church which emphasizes the necessity of good works for salvation would find in Mary a supreme example of human merit. Notwithstanding her exalted position in Catholicism, Mary was a human being and like any believer, she performed works of righteousness during her lifetime. However, the words of Isaiah 64:6 apply to her, the same as to all mankind, *"All our righteousnesses are as filthy rags."* Mary's suffering therefore could make no contribution to the redemption of the world. With no support from God's Word, the Catholic Church in numerous papal encyclicals has loaded Mary with every honor, unrestrainedly exalting her power and excellency, thereby laying the foundation on which has been built the great edifice of Mariolatry—the idolatrous worship of Mary. We thank God for Mary, a wonderful woman of faith and obedience to God. Elizabeth in her greeting said, "Blessed is she that believed".

For centuries, Satan has been using a counterfeit Mary to deceive millions of devout Catholics. Deception was the device he used in the Garden of Eden when he tempted Eve and it is the device he uses today. The Bible, in 2 Corinthians 11:14, tells us that Satan comes as an angel of light. Examples of this are apparitions at places like Lourdes and Fatima. People are called to pray the rosary, do penance, make reparation to Mary's "Immaculate" heart. Only faith in Jesus Christ can save us, there is nothing we can do apart from Him that has eternal value. These messages are lies of Satan, twisting the truth of the Gospel. The only means of uncovering these deceptions is the Word of God. Jesus Himself dealt with the temptations of Satan in the wilderness by using the words of Scripture (Matthew 4:4, 7, 10).

The Good News

At one of the last provincial assemblies of the order which I attended while still a religious, I remember a Scripture that was read, *"See, I have this day set thee over the nations and over the king-doms, to root out and to pull down, and to destroy and to throw down, to build and to plant"* (Jeremiah 1:10). Jeremiah lived to see this prophecy come true. People world-wide, as they hear the Gospel and look to the Word of God for truth, are able by the grace of God to leave behind religious traditions and unbiblical beliefs long held sacred by themselves, their fathers and their forefathers. New wine has to be put into new wineskins. People are leaving denominational churches, each with its own particular religious laws which only serve to divide the Body of Christ, and coming out into fresh ground to live the Christian life as outlined in the Acts of the Apostles and the Epistles.

In Romans we read of Gentiles, sinners who were not seeking after God but who were made righteous by faith, while the religious Jews who were very zealous, doing everything they could, were not made righteous before God. The religious Jews were zealous but misdirected as it says in Romans 10:2, *"They have a zeal for God, but not according to knowledge."* Some people find it hard to accept salvation as a **gift**. "That makes it too easy", was one comment I heard. And another, "There must be a catch somewhere." Obviously for some, the Good News is too good to be true. That salvation is unmerited and undeserved is the offence of the Gospel. That is what upset the Jews in Jesus' day and what upsets religion today. Religious Jews crucified Christ and persecuted the early Church and it is still religious people today who come out against the Gospel. Good people who want to maintain their own goodness are sometimes hard to reach with the true Gospel. For them, the Good News becomes bad news. If God were to ask us what we had done to entitle us to enter heaven, a true Christian would say it was nothing he had done, but that he had put all his trust in Jesus. An axiom to remember is: "Religion is built on what man does for God. Christianity is built on what God has done for man."

The Great Commission

Before ascending into heaven, Jesus gave the Great Commission to His disciples, "Go into the whole world and preach the Gospel." God has given **us** a ministry of reconciliation and we need to make sure that we ourselves have the true message described in 2 Corinthians 5:17-21. We are not to be engaged in reconciling people to God either by the Sacrament of Reconciliation (Confession) or by any other action of man. Reconciliation is something that happened at the Cross of Calvary. In 2

"We are ambassadors for Christ"

Corinthians 5:20 we read that we are to be **ambassadors for Christ**, His personal representatives, pleading with people to be reconciled to God. God is extending the hand of friendship to us. Will you grasp that Hand, will you believe in what God says His Son did for you on Calvary? Will you repent of your dead works and accept God's gift of righteousness in order to be saved?

To carry out this ministry, Jesus told His first ambassadors to wait until they would be "endued with power from on high". Here Jesus was referring to the baptism in the Holy Spirit, He Himself being the Baptizer. His disciples needed the power of the Holy Spirit that would enable them to preach the Gospel. Like them, we all need the special anointing of the Holy Spirit to help us to carry out our ministry, *"Not by might, nor by power, but by my Spirit saith the Lord of hosts"* (Zechariah 4:6). The Holy Spirit is now here on this earth convicting the world of sin. The sin He is most concerned with is the refusal to believe in Jesus Christ and His work of salvation. Our ministry is to tell the Good News to everyone we can. The price of redemption for all men has been paid. Forgiveness is available to all who will believe. Peace is possible even in this life. It is the responsibility of every believer as an ambassador for Jesus Christ to make known to the world, the Good News of the true Gospel.

The Power of the True Gospel

Ever since I came to know Jesus, my desire has been to share with others about the salvation we have in Jesus. *"There is none good but one, that is God"* (Matthew 19:17). Once we understand this truth, we know we cannot depend on ourselves or any person living or dead. We need Jesus and belief in Him is what God asks of us. My favorite salvation Scripture is what Jesus Himself said to Nicodemus, *"Unless a man is born again he cannot enter into the Kingdom of Heaven."* Being born again and believing in Jesus is therefore one and the same. I had often heard the story of Nicodemus but it took over sixty years for me to understand the message. I had followed the traditions and doctrines of men never asking myself what Jesus meant by the term "born again". Jesus referred Nicodemus to the brazen serpent that was lifted up by Moses in the desert, symbolic of Himself Who would be lifted up on the cross. Believe in Jesus and you will be born again, you will be saved.

The first Christians preached with great power as we are told in the Acts of the Apostles and Paul said that his message was not with wise, persuasive words but with a demonstration of the Spirit's power so that people's faith might not be in men but in the power of God. The Gospel is not only about what Jesus did two thousand years ago but about what He is doing today. It is the power of God to those who believe.

A Message for the Reader

In this testimony, I have taken the opportunity to share some of the truths from God's Word that were unknown to me for years. I wish to conclude by returning to the wonderful message of the true Gospel. It is a simple message, yet one that is hidden from millions of people today. The Gospel is the story of the power of the precious blood of Jesus, shed for you on the cross at Calvary, "The Story of the Great Exchange", God's righteousness for our sins! *For he hath made him, who knew no sin, to be sin for us, that we might be made the righteousness of God in him"* (2 Corinthians 5:21).

Dear reader, the moment you are convicted of your sin and see that there is no way to save yourself, that salvation is only possible by believing in the finished work of Jesus Christ—His death, burial and resurrection—is the moment of your salvation. You can know for certain that heaven is yours for all eternity. It is the grace of God made available to us as a gift that is received by faith, *"while we were yet sinners, Christ died for us"* (Romans 5:8). God is faithful to all who seek Him, *"a broken and a contrite heart, O God thou wilt not despise"* (Psalm 51:17).

"Whosoever shall call on the name of the Lord shall be saved" (Acts 2:21).

19

Karlene Lynn

All I Wanted to Know Was to Know Jesus

A few months before she went to be with her Savior, in May of 1995, Karlene Lynn wrote her testimony. Pastor Mike Gendron led her to the Lord, baptized, discipled and buried her. Karlene died just eighteen months after receiving the gift of salvation. She had been a nun for ten years and during all that time had neither heard the Gospel nor opened the Bible. After Vatican Counsel II (1962-1965) made some recommendations modifying the restrictions that surrounded the daily life of nuns, she saw how unimportant a religious life was to the nuns around her and almost had a nervous breakdown. These people were secular in nature, although in nuns' robes. Eventually, she wrote a letter to Pope John Paul II asking for a dispensation from her vows as a nun. A letter granting her wish was received during the summer of 1967. She left the convent life and went to Cedar Rapids, Iowa, where she found a job teaching in the local schools as a fifth grade teacher.

This is her story as she wrote it and as it was read by Pastor Gendron at her funeral. The introduction here and the Scripture verses, which clarify the truth that both assured her of eternal life with her Lord and prepared her for it, have been added.

Why I Wrote My Testimony

I am fifty-five years old and have been battling cancer for seven years. I feel compelled to write this testimony before I die, which I understand should be soon. I was a Catholic for fifty-three and a

"As a nun"

half years and a nun for ten years. I was saved by the grace of God eighteen months ago.

My First Contact With Truth

One day I met Pastor Mike Gendron, who directs a worldwide evangelistic outreach to Roman Catholics called Proclaiming the Gospel. He was handing out evangelistic literature specifically written for Catholics. As a Catholic, I never felt a need to read any of his publications because I believed I was already going to heaven. I never ever owned a Bible until just recently. After all, I was a Catholic, I didn't need one. In fact during the whole ten years I was in the convent with over two hundred other nuns, we had one Bible among us but we never opened it. I do remember during my ten years in the convent, all I ever wanted was to know Jesus. I just never knew how easy it was to know Him. The Bible was so close, yet we were discouraged to read it on our own.

A Clear Contrast

The Holy Spirit didn't give up on me. Weeks later we were invited to a small group meeting for Bible study, prayer and fellowship. Mike shared the Gospel with me and encouraged me to read a publication that showed the difference between what the Catholic Bible teaches and what a Catholic catechism teaches. When I read it, I became angry at him for making my church look bad. Little did I know, he only wanted me to make a choice between trusting in the Word of God rather than the teachings of men for my salvation. He knew it was impossible for anyone to believe both. *"No man can serve two masters; for either he will hate the one, and love the other; or else he will hold to the one, and despise the other"* (Matthew 6: 24).

It was because of Mike's explanation and approaching me to examine the wrongs of "my faith" that I realized I was not saved. This gave me a new desire to pursue Christianity, leave the Catholic

Church and receive Jesus as my personal Savior. *"I am the way, the truth, and the life; no man cometh unto the Father, but by me"*(John 14:6). *"Verily, verily, I say unto you, He that heareth my word and believeth on him that sent me, hath everlasting life, and shall not come into judgment, but is passed from death unto life"* (John 5:24).

"As a Bible Believer with my husband and two daughters"

Shortly thereafter, Pastor Mike baptized me as my public confession of my faith. I knew that my baptism as an infant was a meaningless ritual. I always begged God to let me find Jesus and to be used by Him. He granted me that wish and I am now a Christian, saved by the precious blood of my Savior.

Redemption Through His Blood

"Blessed be the God and Father of our Lord Jesus Christ, who hath blessed us with all spiritual blessings in heavenly places in Christ....In whom we have redemption through his blood, the forgiveness of sins, according to the riches of his grace." (Ephesians 1:3-7)

Believer's Baptism

"We are buried with him by baptism into death, that as Christ was raised up from the dead by the glory of the Father, even so we also should walk in newness of life." (Romans 6: 4)

My Dying Prayer

I'm on death's door. I am ready to go be with Jesus. He has called me and I have received Him. Pastor Mike will soon officiate at my "going home" celebration. My prayer now is for the salvation of my Catholic family who will be attending my funeral. I pray my death will bring them life as the wonderful news of my Savior is proclaimed. Then they, too, can know Jesus and receive His most precious gift of eternal life! *"I am the resurrection and the life; he that believeth in me, though he were dead, yet he shall live"* (John 11: 25).

20

Helene Hart

From Confusion to the Truth of Scripture

Family Life

As I look back over the years I realize now how the grace of God was evident in my life. I'm the oldest of eleven children. Although there was not much money, our daily needs were always met by loving and supportive parents. Being a close family, we often spent the evenings playing games and enjoying one another's company. There was always enough warmth and love for everyone.

As a family, we believed in God and tried our best to please Him with our sincerity and good deeds. Also, praying the rosary daily was a vital part of our lives. However, Bible reading was never stressed at home or in Church.

The Convent

At age fourteen, I entered a boarding school exclusively for girls. During this time, I realized I wanted to become a nun. At age seventeen, I entered the convent and one year later was teaching first grade. My first ten years in the convent were happy and exciting and I felt I could not do enough for the Lord. There was never an idle moment. My time was filled with praying, teaching, counseling, and visiting the sick. Every day of convent life was busy and challenging. Eventually I was promoted to principal and taught seventh and eight grade. I felt that God was very pleased with all my good deeds.

Confusion and Anger

During this time, however, God used the young people in my religious education class to challenge me by asking questions about the Catholic faith which I could not answer. I began to search for answers, but there was no one to help me. As a result, I began questioning some of the Catholic Church's doctrines and teachings. I had particular difficulty accepting ecclesiastical dogmas which could change with the passing of time. I am speaking of man-made church laws that could send a person to hell (mortal sin) but that subsequently may be rescinded. The lingering question that always surfaced in my mind was what happened to all the souls that died during the dispensation of this ordinance? Was this God's justice? It did not seem fair to me. Additionally, I had serious problems confessing my sins to a priest when I believed in my heart I could go straight to the Lord. Moreover, I reasoned why pray to Mary and the saints when it was God who answers prayers.

Having no one to confide in and help me with my quest for spiritual truth, I became increasingly upset and confused. Consequently, I was very unhappy and officially asked to leave convent life.

The Church responded by insisting I see a psychiatrist and spend some time in the convent infirmary. I could not accept this. So, after eighteen years, I left the community life only after being told I would lose my soul and go to Hell. I was disillusioned, confused, and very angry with the Church to which I had given my entire life.

New Life

In 1971, I met a man who eventually became my husband. He was the first person I had ever dated. He was a caring and understanding man who helped me through the emotional traumas I had experienced. Five years after we were married, we had a beautiful baby girl. However, several months later my doctors informed me I would have to have brain surgery. The operation was a success and once again I knew there was a wonderful God who loved and cared for me.

Things began to change in my life when I met a neighbor who was a born again Christian. I was invited to attend a weekly Bible study. The lingering questions, the doubts and fears I had over the years were beginning to be answered through the Bible. During one of these visits, I realized I needed to put all of my faith and trust in

Jesus Christ and in His completed work of salvation on the cross of Calvary. In John 3:16, the Scripture states, *"For God so loved the world, that He gave His only begotten Son, that whosoever believeth in Him should not perish, but have everlasting life."* And in 1 Peter 3:18, *"For Christ also hath once suffered for sins, the just for the unjust, that he might bring us to God."* That day I believed what God's word says, I trusted on Jesus and Him alone and was saved! For the first time in my life I was completely trusting Christ for my salvation and not my religious works or merits. God revealed from His Word in Ephesians 2:8-9 this was what He wanted me to do. It says, *"For by grace are ye saved through faith; and that not of yourselves: it is the gift of God: Not of works, lest any man should boast."*

After I was saved, problems surfaced in our marriage. My husband resented me being saved and attending a Bible-believing church. For the next three years, the situation was extremely tense and difficult. However, the Holy Spirit began dealing with my husband's heart. While I attended church services on Sunday evenings, he began watching Gospel services on television. God revealed to him what He had made clear to me through the Scriptures—personal salvation is in Jesus Christ and not in a church. Soon thereafter my husband also called upon Jesus to save him.

Truth Replaces Confusion

Once we were both saved, God began to heal our marriage. Moreover, the roadblocks preventing true peace of mind and happiness in our marriage were eventually replaced with the things of God. Today, there is love, peace and joy in my life with a wonderful husband and daughter. We are serving the Lord together and have a happy family life. Daily we spend time together in prayer and Bible reading. The Lord has blessed us abundantly and I give Him all the praise, honor and glory! Since I have been saved and born again I have claimed Jeremiah 33:3 as my life's verse, *"Call upon me, and I will answer thee, and shew thee great and mighty things, which thou knowest not."*

The many questions I pondered as a nun have all been answered from the Scriptures. I trust that by my testimony, your eyes will be opened to the truth of God's Word. As we read through the New Testament, we notice Jesus commands His disciples to preach the Gospel of salvation. All the Gospel writers affirm that Jesus stated our faith must be firmly placed in Him. He never instructed anyone to have faith in a church. No church is able to take sins away. As a Catholic, I was spiritually lost because I was trusting in my church and good deeds to help me earn salvation and merit the favor of God. I had never trusted Christ to be my all sufficient Saviour. As Christians, our trust is grounded not in what we are doing for Jesus, but in what He has done for us. When Jesus died on Calvary, He said, *"It is finished."* His redemptive work was complete. He died for us because we can do nothing to save ourselves. Once you recognize that you are a sinner and can only be saved by Jesus Christ, *"Believe on the Lord Jesus Christ and Thou shalt be saved"* (Acts 16:31). *"For He* [God, the Father] *hath made Him* [Jesus Christ] *to be sin for us, Who knew no sin; that we might be made the righteousness of God in Him"* (II Corinthians 5:21). My friend, Jesus is willing and able to save you **today**!

Epilogue

Is the Convent Life Biblical?

As you read this book, you will have seen that all who entered the convent thought that such a state of life was godly. It is important to understand why they held this presupposition as truth.

The teaching of the Roman Catholic Church (RCC) is quite clear regarding the "religious form of life". Their official statement declares unequivocally, "Besides giving legal sanction to the religious form of life and thus raising it to the dignity of a canonical state, the Church sets it forth liturgically also as a state of consecration to God. She herself, in virtue of her God-given authority, receives the vows of those who profess this form of life...."[1]

Enticing the Young

The Roman Catholic system's primary tactic is to whet the appetite of her youths' zeal and idealism by such dramatic words as,

The profound meaning of obedience is revealed in the fullness of this mystery of death and resurrection in which the supernatural destiny of man is brought to realization in a perfect manner. It is in fact through sacrifice, suffering and death that man attains true life. Exercising authority in the midst of your brethren means therefore being their servants, in accordance with the example of him who gave 'his life as a ransom for many.'[2]

---

1. *Vatican Council II: The Conciliar and Post Conciliar Documents,* No. 28, "Lumen Gentium", 21 November 1964, Austin Flannery, O.P., General Editor, 2 vols. (Costello Publishing Co., Northport, New York, 1975 & 1982) Vol. I, Para. 45, p. 406.

2. Flannery, No. 53, S.C.R.S.I., *Evangelica Testificatio,* 29 June 1971, Vol. I, Para. 24, p. 691.

The sentiment and feeling of sentences such as this one, "…It is in fact through sacrifice, suffering and death that man attains true life…", led many of the women in this book to enter the convent. That souls can be saved through the penitential work of other human beings has been Satan's message consistently in the cults and pagan religions. It appeals to a person's spiritual pride—even in the convent. "…Ye shall be as gods…" (Genesis 3:5) was the message of Satan's original lie, and thus the theme continues.

One of the very subtle ways the Roman Catholic system entices young women into the "religious state" is by declaring that by making public vows, a young woman is able through the Roman Catholic institution to consecrate herself to God "until death". "Religious profession" is defined by Canon 654,

> By religious profession members assume by public vow the observance of the three evangelical counsels, are consecrated to God through the ministry of the Church, and are incorporated into the institute with rights and duties defined by law.[3]

Close reading show that this is a very subtle way of offering to a young woman a substitute for marriage, a substitute which purportedly would make her as an individual very special and, like marriage, incorporate her into a publicly acceptable state "with rights and duties". It is declared that the members are thus "consecrated to God". As the Roman Catholic laws regarding Religious life unfold, however, it becomes clear that the young woman's consecration was not to God but rather to the Roman Catholic Church[4], and that in this state she is, in fact, special to no one.

"Evangelical counsels" explained

The Roman Church tries to justify the religious form of life which she herself has set up by declaring that "the evangelical counsels of chaste self-dedication to God, of poverty and of obedience"[5] are part of the teaching and example of Christ Himself. The use of the word "counsel" in the RCC context is based on the

---

3. *Code of Canon Law* Latin-English Ed. (Washington, DC 20064: Canon Law Society of America, 1983). All references to canon law are taken from this volume.

4. If this were not so, how else could Canon 701 be explained, "Vows, rights and obligations derived from profession cease ipso facto by legitimate dismissal…" If one's vows truly consecrated one to God, no human "legitimate dismissal" could cause them to cease "ipso facto".

5. Flannery, No. 28, "Lumen Gentium", Vol. I, Para. 43, p. 402.

parable of the rich young ruler (Mt. 19:21). The biblical thrust of the parable is that Christ, knowing the pride of the young man, answered him in such a way as to expose to him his hypocrisy. The Catholic interpretation, however, twists the meaning of the parable to say that Christ's counsel to the young man was to do a good work which, rather than commanded, He commended him to do. According to Roman Catholic understanding, if he followed Christ's commendation, he would be following a way of greater perfection of holiness. On this basis the RCC justifies setting up her monastic system which defines the "evangelical counsels" specifically. Such thinking asserts that something (in this case celibacy, poverty, and obedience to the RCC) can be added to the moral law to allow one to achieve a more perfect state.[6] Such teaching flies in the face of the perfect, finished atonement of Christ and His righteousness imputed to the believer as the perfect, finished covering.

A Controlling Poverty

In return for swearing fidelity to the counsel or vow of poverty, a nun is promised complete economic security by the Roman Catholic Church. In such a state of poverty, she may own nothing but, usually as a corporate member of the community, she is endowed with material goods. This circumvention interferes with the biblical pattern of responsibility of personal ownership, as well as the spiritual maturation acquired when a person trusts God for daily bread.

A Question of Authority

Christ Jesus lived in the world, but was not of the world. He was absolutely obedient to His Father, even as the believer is told to be obedient to Him and to His Word, *"My sheep know My voice."* *"Whoever loves Me will keep My word."*

A nun's vow of obedience, however, brings in a concept alien to biblical thought. Canon 601 teaches,

> The evangelical counsel of obedience, undertaken in a spirit of faith and love in the following of Christ who was obedient even unto death requires a submission of the will

---

6. For an excellent discussion of this point, see Francis Turretin, *Institutes of Elenctic Theology,* James T. Dennison, Jr., Ed., Tr. by George Musgrave Giger (Phillipsburg, NJ 08865-0817: Presbyterian & Reformed Publishing, 1994), Vol. II, Question 4, pp. 28-30.

to legitimate superiors, who stand **in the place of God** when they command according to the proper constitutions." (Emphasis added)

Obedience to the Lord commanded in the Bible is turned here in the Catholic world into obedience to one's local superior "who stands in the place of God". In Matthew 23, the Lord utterly condemned the Pharisees who were heading in that idolatrous direction when they sought to be called "Father" or "Master" by the people. Though the Pharisees imposed burdens on the people, they never came anywhere near to declaring a submission to "superiors, who stand in the place of God". The Catholic Church, however, declares, "Likewise, Religious are obliged to observe all those prescriptions which episcopal councils or conferences legitimately decree as binding on all.[7] And she enforces the same standard, "Religious can be coerced by penalties by the local ordinary in all matters in which they are subject to him." (Canon 1320) Such dictates as these run contrary to the Lord's command to His servants, *"Stand fast therefore in the liberty wherewith Christ hath made us free, and be not entangled again with the yoke of bondage"* (Galatians 5:1).

An Illegal Pattern Imposed

The Roman Catholic system must have new blood in each generation. Nuns are the backbone of the Catholic parochial schools and of the Catholic hospitals, both of which institutions having been proven to be places in which many Protestants are converted to Catholicism.[8] Thus the Roman Catholic Church seeks to circumvent the vows of marriage by requiring fidelity to her own definition of "chaste self-dedication", thereby instituting celibacy as the required state for the Religious. The Roman system presses egregiously on the idealism and zeal of her young women by declaring untruthfully,

> ...Furthermore the religious state constitutes a closer imitation and an abiding reenactment in the Church of the

---

7. Flannery, No. 92, S.C.R.S.I., *Mutuae Relationes*, April 1978, Vol. II, Para. 44, p. 235.

8. For records from the past, see "Bishop Brute's Report to Rome in 1836" in *Documentary Reports on Early American Catholicism*, Philip Gleason, Ed. (New York, NY: Arno Press Inc., 1978) pp. 229-231. Bishop Brute reports that in the conversion of Protestants two of the main avenues of conversion are through Protestant children being sent to Catholic schools, and through hospitalization of Protestants who are in danger of death. The same is still true today.

form of life which the Son of God made his own when he came into the world to do the will of the Father and which he propounded to the disciples who followed him.[9]

To assert that Christ made the Religious state (i.e., the monastic system) "his own and he propounded it to his disciples" is a falsehood which flatly denies the historical facts. Nowhere in Scripture does He "make it his own" nor "propound it to his disciples".

Some may attempt to rationalize the Roman Catholic position by saying that culturally monasticism was not known in the Lord's time; however, the Essenes at Qumran lived in monastic fashion then. It is clear from the Bible that the Lord neither lived in a monastery, nor gave any hint of setting up such a way of life, nor instructed His disciples in that way of life.

According to the Lord's teaching, believers are sanctified by the work of the Holy Spirit in applying the Biblical Word of Truth, not by trying to escape the world. In John 17:15, Jesus prays, *"I pray not that thou shouldest take them out of the world, but that Thou shouldest keep them from the evil one." "Sanctify them through thy truth: thy word is truth"* (verse 17). Yet official Roman Catholic teaching declares,

> Life consecrated by the profession of the evangelical counsels is a stable form of living by which [the] faithful, following Christ **more closely** under the action of the Holy Spirit, are totally dedicated to God...[10] (Emphasis added)

The words "more closely" therefore, contrast to the vows of marriage, the meaning is that consecrated life is a closer following of Christ than is marriage. Clearly, God has never declared this to be so.

The Bible declares to all true believers, *"But ye are a chosen generation, a royal priesthood, a holy nation, a peculiar people; that ye should shew forth the praises of him who hath called you out of darkness into his marvelous light"* (1 Peter 2:9). The gift of celibacy is given only to a few. The time and circumstances of that celibate life are solely between the Lord and the individual. (Matthew 19:12) It is in this exact context that the Lord speaks of the eunuchs for the kingdom of heaven's sake. It is to be noted in this case that there is no new institution authorized; rather, *"...He that is able to receive it, let him receive it."* It is in the stability of the family life established by the Lord that an individual with God's gift of celibacy may

---

9. Flannery, No. 28, "Lumen Gentium", Vol. I, Para. 44, p. 404.
10. Canon 573, Sect. 1.

The Truth Set Us Free

attempt to live out his calling. What the Lord did NOT say was this: "for this cause shall a man also leave father and mother and join himself to a group of other celibates, and their way of life shall be established." No such form of life was ever established by the Lord.

Putting the Lord as absolutely first in relationships is what the Lord has taught again and again, *"He that loveth father or mother more than me is not worthy of me: and he that loveth son or daughter more than me is not worthy of me."*[11] Thus the leaving of house, parents, brethren, wife, or children for His sake is what every believer must do. Nothing and no one is to become more precious to any of the believers than He is. But that such living does not constitute a religious house is made absolutely clear by the Lord's promise to believers now in the world, *"But he shall receive an hundredfold now in this time, houses, and brethren, and sisters, and mothers, and children, and lands, with persecutions;..."* (Mark 10:30).

These very relationships are deepened and more properly realized in the midst of persecution on account of the Lord. Again, God's Word is clear and precise. Had the Lord envisaged convents with Mother Superiors and Father Generals, He would have said so in this context. The hundredfold that is given to the believer is of the same fabric of what God Himself has ordained. There is no hint of a separate "stable form of living" or of "following Christ more closely." To decree that there is such is to denigrate marriage.

No "mystical espousal"

Sometimes the basic understanding is not only that Religious life is a "closer following of Christ," but the idea is also given that it is a mystical union with Christ. An example of this double assertion of superiority is the text of "The Consecrated Life and Its Role in the Church and in the World",

> ...Similar to these forms of consecrated life is the order of virgins, who, hearkening to the sacred call to follow Christ more closely, are consecrated to God by the diocesan bishop according to the approved liturgical rite; are mystically espoused to Christ, Son of God; and are dedicated to the service of the Church...[12]

---

11. Matthew 10:37.

12. "The Consecrated Life: Excerpts from the Lineamenta for the 9th Ordinary General Assembly of the Synod of Bishops", *Catholic International*, (Brighton, MA 02135: North American Province of the Augustinians of the Assumption) Vol. 4, No. 2, February, 1993, p. 58. English text as published by the Libreria Editrice Vaticana, Vatican City.

188

Here the words " more closely" contrast to the vows of marriage ordained in His written Word; but the second claim, that such "an order of virgins" are "mystically espoused to Christ" is simply not true. In the Bible, the Lord rejoices over all born of the Spirit as a bridegroom rejoices over the bride. To go beyond what God Himself has instituted is sin. The biblical admonition is straightforward, *"...not to think above that which is written"* (I Corinthians 4:6).

The Real Call

By nature, every person is born a sinner destined for Hell. Salvation comes through Jesus Christ alone. The real call of Scripture is to believe on the Lord Jesus Christ alone, for it is by grace alone through faith alone that a person is born again to new life in Christ. *"The Father loveth the Son, and hath given all things into His hand. He that believeth on the Son hath everlasting life: and he that believeth not the Son shall not see life; but the wrath of God abideth on him."*[13]

The Convent

If you are in the convent and understand that salvation is by grace alone and that you must depend only on the righteousness of Christ Jesus alone, perhaps you now can see why thousands left monasteries and convents at the time of the Reformation. You may know very well the Catholic law, "Those who have legitimately left a religious institution or have been legitimately dismissed from one can request nothing from it for any work done in it...."[14]

From inside the system, it looks impossible to face any future, for not only can one leave with "nothing from it for any work done" but often one leaves with the disapproval of family and friends. This is the point at which these testimonies to the faithfulness of the Lord become doubly precious. The Father's love is personal; He calls them individual by individual. He calls you by name and provides for you. He, the mighty God, the Father, says to you, *"Wherefore come out from among them, and be ye separate, saith the Lord, and touch not the unclean thing; and I will receive you, And will be a Father unto you, and ye shall be my sons and daughters, saith the Lord Almighty"* (II Corinthians 6:17-18).

Although you quite probably are aware of the huge obstacles that stand before you, like those which were faced by Peggy

---

13. John 3:35-36.
14. Canon 702.

O'Neill, Mary Ann Pakiz, and Eileen Donnelly, the word of the Lord is clear and the evidence of His gracious presence in the lives of those who truly have been born again is indisputable, "For He hath said, 'I will never leave thee nor forsake thee.' So that we may boldly say, The Lord is my helper, and I will not fear what man shall do unto me" (Hebrews 13:5-6).

RICHARD BENNETT, September, 1997

To order additional copies of

The Truth Set Us Free:
Twenty Former Nuns Tell Their Stories

please send $12.95* per copy
(shipping and handling included in USA,
Canadian orders add $2.00 US) to:

Richard Bennett
PO Box 55353
Portland, OR 97238

or to order by credit card please call

1-800-917-BOOK

*Quantity Discounts are Available